VALDEMARS BLANKENBURGS 1907 - 1991

KIELDER CAMERA

This book is dedicated to those, past and … kenburgs, were inspired by this unique part of Britai… ndscapes and people, and to those who dedicated … ces into preserving their work and making it accessib…

The story of Valdemars Blankenburgs can now be told thanks to historians, photographers, archivists at the Northumberland Records Office, and the tireless volunteers of the Heritage Centre in Bellingham, particularly Steve Gibbon, Stan Owen and Wesley Turnbull.

This book could not have been written without the help and encouragement of the three children of Valdemars and Elfrida Blankenburgs, especially Maija, who has supplied so much information, inspiration and encouragement.

Front cover: Valdemars Blankenburgs with his camera.

VALDEMARS BLANKENBURGS 1907 - 1991

KIELDER CAMERA

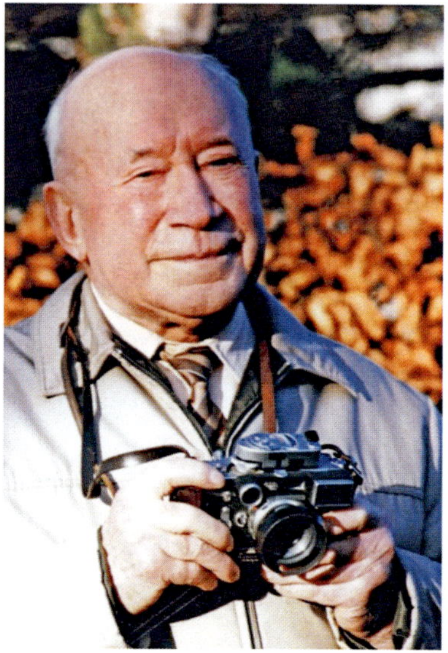

Valdemars Blankenburgs is the subject of this book. This is the story of a Latvian who lost almost everything during the course of the Second World War and who left his native land as a refugee to seek a new life for himself and his family in Great Britain. It is the fascinating story of the determination of one man, his will to succeed and his love of the Forest.

His story begins in December 1947 when he started working as a surveyor for the Forestry Commission at Kielder and when his life, changed firstly by war, was changed again by walking the hills of Kielder.

The portrait of his life is painted in the following pages but Kielder is the place that frames his portrait and it will be in order to give a brief history of the Kielder that he found upon his arrival in Great Britain.

CONTENTS

APPENDICES

HOW THE NORTH TYNE VALLEY CHANGED

The most tangible reminder of former occupants of the North Tyne Valley is the Devil's Lapful, a Neolithic long cairn, dating to around 3,000 BC, to be found one kilometre south-east of Kielder. It is one of the few surviving long cairns in Northumberland, constructed of rounded boulders with some stone slabs and with smaller stones at the edges. It measures 60 by 14 metres and is 2 metres high. There has been some later quarrying to make a sheep fold, which is next to the cairn on the north-west. Such a monument probably marked the burial site for a local community over several generations and this community would have consisted of shepherds who would become the most numerous occupants of the North Tyne Valley and its lonely hills.

The valley of the North Tyne, however, would change more than any other valley in Northumberland. The driving force behind this change has been a series of "invasions" of which those who created Kielder Forest and Kielder Reservoir were the last, bringing changes in population and shifting the focus from sheep farming alone.

BORDER REIVERS

It began in medieval times with the Border Reivers, powerful families and clans, who, in the absence of law and order, would regularly attack their neighbours for the purpose of pillage and often to avenge past wrongs that had passed from one generation to the next. To protect themselves in those troubled times, householders built fortified houses, called bastles or peles, where they could barricade themselves against an imminent attack: animals on the ground floor and humans on the upper storey. The years of warfare gradually died out after 1707 with the Acts of Union between England and Scotland and many farmhouses in the North Tyne Valley date from the more settled times of the later 18th century, either built from scratch or converted from peles. The exploits of the Border Reivers survive in the lore and legend of Northumberland.

RAILWAY NAVVIES

Between 1855 and 1862, hundreds of Navvies built the Border Counties Railway, a single track line of 42 miles, connecting Hexham in Northumberland with Riccarton Junction on the Waverley Route in Roxburghshire. It opened up the remote parts of the North Tyne Valley and provided routes for trade and tourism, especially members of the hunting, shooting and fishing fraternity, who paid good money for the sport along the River North Tyne, such as on the Mounces Estate of the Swinburne family of Capheaton Hall. The area was patrolled by a corps of gamekeepers and water bailiffs.

The anticipated level of commercial traffic, however, especially coal from the Plashetts coal field, did not materialise and the sparse population produced very little local passenger traffic except on market and show days. The single track never fulfilled its potential as a direct route between Newcastle and Edinburgh and it was often unfairly described as the railway that led from nowhere to nowhere. The line closed to passengers in 1956 and completely in 1958 when the Border Counties Bridge near Hexham was demolished. The foundations of the bridge and the changing currents of the River Tyne at this point had always made this a weak link in the line.

PLASHETTS MINERS

The promoters of the railway had vested interests in the commercial exploitation of coal at Plashetts Colliery, hidden in the hills between Falstone and Kielder, which operated between 1862 and the mid-1930s. The hills around Plashetts were full of coal, the "black diamonds" upon which Victorian society relied for almost everything, and the success of the mine was toasted on 20th May 1861 in the pure water from the Belling Burn, which ran alongside the original drift, aptly named Seldom Seen.

Living in splendid isolation, 750 feet above sea level, the miners and their families came from a wide geographical area, though many came from across the Border as pits in southern Scotland closed. There was no road access to Plashetts. Goods, food, people, the living and dead, everyone and everything, in fact, were carried along a wagonway originally built to serve the Seldom Seen drift. There was a chapel, school and shop but no doctor, priest, or policeman. The people of Plashetts seem to have lived peaceful but hard lives, united by the coal that brought them together and lay all around.

The miners supported the General Strike of 1926 but many of the drifts became flooded. Plashetts was never the same again and output dwindled as the miners gradually drifted away to find alternative jobs. The final blow came on 29th August 1932 when Joseph Slater, the owner and manager, was fatally overcome by black damp gas while inspecting one of the drifts. Mining at Plashetts officially ceased a couple of years later but a few men still continued to mine the coal that remained in those hills, albeit on a very small scale, with the last drift closing in 1992.

KIELDER FORESTERS

As one door was closing in the mine, another had opened in the forest. In the same year, 1926, as the General Strike was staged, planting began at Smale Farm, a couple of miles west of Falstone as the crow flies and six miles from Plashetts. In the beginning, results were disappointing but improved planting techniques, involving digging a shallow ditch and planting the saplings on a platform of upturned turf, were extremely encouraging. Locals were employed in this enterprise, including some of the miners still working at Plashetts but who, with an eye to their future prospects, were seeking alternative employment in the area. The planting at Smale might have come to nothing, had it not been for the determination of Roy Robinson and another timely opportunity.

The 8th Duke of Northumberland died in 1930, just a few years after his father, the 7th Duke, had died in 1918. The two deaths, taking place within a relatively short time, had incurred heavy death duties. Faced with this unexpected tax burden, the family decided to sell their 47,000-acre Kielder Estate to the Forestry Commission and received £105,000 to mitigate their tax liability. This enabled the Forestry Commission to extend planting from 1932 and create what has become Kielder Forest.

A similar opportunity also occurred in 1932 with the death of Sir James Marr, the wealthy Sunderland Shipbuilder, who had purchased over 8,000 acres of land in Upper Redesdale from Lord Redesdale in 1918. The Forestry Commission purchased this land as well, which became the foundation of the 17,000 acre Redesdale Forest that was itself an extension of their Kielder and Wark Forests in North Tynedale.

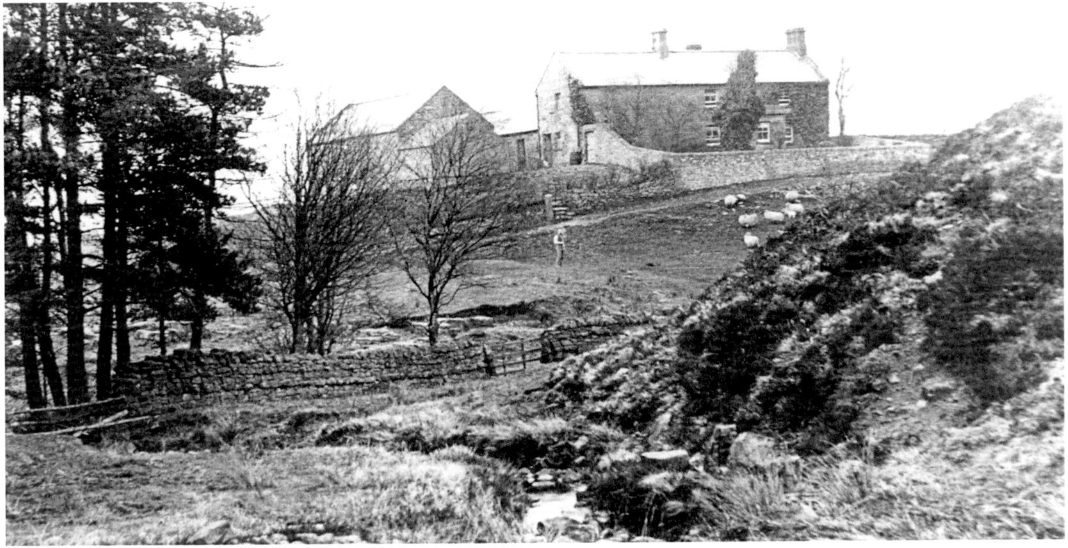

The Archive Postcards of the North Tyne

SMALE FARM Situated two miles west of Stannersburn, the farm of the Murray family became in 1926 the birthplace of Kielder Forest when the Forestry Commission leased 45 acres of land on which to begin the trial planting of conifers. Results were not encouraging at first because saplings were planted directly into the ground which was of poor quality and oxygen starved. It was found, however, that they grew well if planted on a platform of soil which also protected them from weeds and flooding.

LONG-TERM UNEMPLOYED "DOLIES"

Additional unskilled labour for the planting of Kielder Forest came from the Government Instructional Centre, which opened, complete with its own railway halt, just south of Kielder at Lewiefield in 1933. These Labour Camps were built nationwide in the 1930s and offered "rehabilitation" courses to the long-term unemployed. At Kielder, 200 trainees attended a 12-week course which taught them the basic manual skills to improve their employment prospects: these included digging ditches, putting up fences and preparing the land for forestry roads. Most trainees benefited from better food than they could afford back home, sporting competitions and visiting concert parties. Others were less positive and occasional "mutinies" broke out over poor standards of accommodation, the lack of amenities and the isolation of their surroundings.

Drunken behaviour was occasionally reported in Hawick, which, thanks to the railway, was a favourite place for a Saturday day out. Many missed the last train home either because they were too drunk or were already sleeping it off in the police cells.

All the Labour Camps were closed at the start of the Second World War and the facilities were put to other purposes. Between 1939 and 1941, Kielder Camp briefly housed Canadian lumberjacks from Newfoundland and then the site was commissioned by the Royal Navy. At the end of the War, the camp housed Displaced Persons and Volunteer Workers from Europe. After the camp closed in 1953, it was used by the Forestry Commission. An active and well-equipped Auxiliary Fire Service used several of the huts to train their volunteers, who were mostly miners from the Northumberland pits.

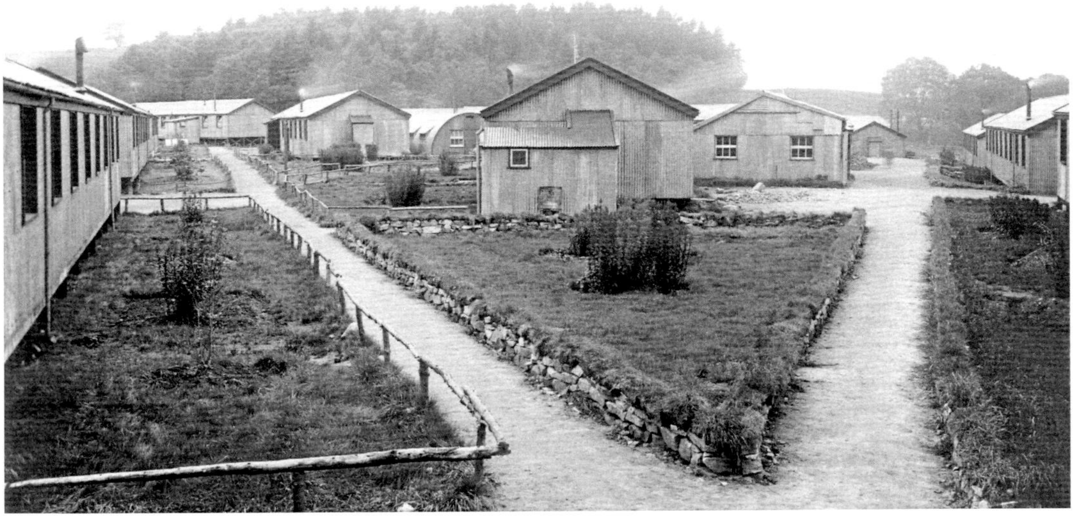

The Archive Postcards of the North Tyne

W. P. COLLIER (1875-1937) was a Bellingham photographer who had a small shop in Lock-Up Lane between 1912 and 1937. Almost on a daily basis, he would ride his motorcycle and take thousands of photographs of Northumberland, which he turned into postcards. This is one of several postcards of Kielder Instructional Centre while it was still occupied by the long-term unemployed, locally known as Dolies. He produced a similar series of postcards of the summer camps at Whickhope and Byrness.

RESERVOIR CONSTRUCTION WORKERS

The final population change came in the 1970s when construction workers came to build Kielder Reservoir, many of whom were housed in a compound on the south side of the rising earth embankment that formed the wall of the dam around two miles from Falstone. This was a large community and the glow from the lighting could be seen all along the valley. Some locals feared that the 20th century construction workers would be like the 19th century navvies who had a reputation for drink-fuelled arguments, especially at the Black Cock Inn at Falstone, but nothing of the sort happened with these workers. After six years of construction, the workers left, the area was landscaped and the new Reservoir was officially opened by Queen Elizabeth II on 26th May 1982. The water authorities appointed a liaison officer and produced a regular broadsheet to keep locals informed of developments but there was a good deal of opposition to the scheme from those whose farms and houses would be submerged. Shepherds, in particular, who had been brought up on the open hills, found it hard to reconcile themselves to the prospect of living in the small houses on offer at Falstone.

Those who are drawn to the activities offered by Kielder Water are often unaware of the history that lies beneath the waves. In the words of the *Kielder Kelpie (2022):*

So, when on Kielder's shore you gaze
O'er waters grey and cold,
Just think about the farms below
And shepherd folk of old.

HOW KIELDER FOREST BEGAN 1919-1926

In 1919, the same year as the Treaty of Versailles was signed, the 12-year-old Valdemars Blankenburgs and his older brother were making his first camera out of German cigar boxes in Latvia. The same year also saw the creation of the Forestry Commission in England to stabilise and expand the production of timber that had been severely depleted during the Great War, notably for pit props, crates, fences, dugouts, bridges and other fortifications. In fact, the UK was the least afforested country in Europe and the demand for wood was desperate. Pit props were essential for miners to dig the coal that powered every aspect of British industry and hence the War Effort.

Seven years later, 1926, when Valdemars was enrolling as a student in the Latvian State Forestry Academy, planting was beginning, under the auspices of Roy Lister Robinson, at Smale Farm near Falstone, North Tyne, signalling what would later become Kielder Forest. Initial results at Smale Farm were not encouraging and, had it not been for the dogged determination of Roy Robinson to see the project succeed, Kielder Forest might never have taken off. A subtle change in planting, however, solved the problem. It was found that, if a shallow trench was dug and the young saplings were planted on the upcast from this trench, the saplings would survive, clear of weeds and water.

Results exceeded expectations and, some 22 years later, Valdemars would be taking a picture of Sir Roy Lister Robinson OBE, now First Baron Robinson of Kielder Forest and of Adelaide, felling one of the first trees to be planted at Smale Farm.

THE FOREST EXPANDS 1932-1939

Tree planting might have stalled at Smale Farm but two unexpected turns of Fate came along in 1932 that boosted the prospects for forestry in the North Tyne and Upper Redesdale. A huge advance in the creation of Kielder Forest was the acquisition in 1932 of 47,000 acres of North Tyne land from the Duke of Northumberland, paid in lieu of death duties, and an adjoining parcel of Upper Redesdale land, bought from the executors of the late Sir James Marr, the Sunderland shipping magnate. Labour came additionally from unemployed miners at Plashetts, where production had fallen dramatically following the General Strike of 1926.

In addition, the early 1930s saw the establishment of Government Instructional Centres to "rehabilitate" the long-term unemployed from the industrial cities. Camps were established at various locations in the UK, such as Thetford, Newcastleton and Kielder, especially in those areas where labour was required for forestry. At Kielder, a camp for 150 men was built near Lewisburn, which was furnished with a new railway station, Lewiefield Halt. The 12-week training course involved digging ditches, preparing roads and erecting fences. Summer camps, with fewer facilities, were established at Whickhope and Byrness. All of these camps were closed at the outbreak of the Second World War and most of the records have been lost or destroyed.

The planting of Kielder Forest continued through the 1930s with accommodation for forestry workers being provided in the scattered farmhouses that came into the possession of the Forestry Commission after its acquisition of the Kielder Estate in the North Tyne Valley and Upper Redesdale. Such accommodation was not ideal and it became clear that new houses were required specifically for foresters with families.

In August 1936, therefore, newspapers carried a series of advertisements for Bricklayers and Joiners for Forestry Commission houses at Falstone, Plashetts and Kielder. Top wages and overtime were promised but the phrase "camp on job" underlined the remote location of the building works.

After several delays, caused by bad weather, changes to the original plans and court proceedings brought by the Forestry Commission against the contractor, many of the houses in Castle Drive at Kielder were completed and several families were already in residence when, on 16th March 1939, the Newcastle Evening Chronicle carried the following article under the headline "Durham Workless Miners Turn Foresters":

"Eight workless men will escape from the spectre of permanent unemployment when they move, in the near future, from Durham mining villages to the Forestry Commission's Kielder estate, where they will tend young trees. They are the last of the 32 impoverished families which have been settled on the estate by the Commission as part of its scheme for turning vast areas of Border moorland into forests. The families will be provided with modern, six-roomed houses at a rent of only four shillings a week. The men will be given work planting saplings and weeding and draining the plantations at a wage of 38/- a week with piece rates in addition. They will find the job strenuous at first, since many of them have been unemployed for some time, one for eight years, and only one has worked on the land before. But, when they get used to it, there will be plenty to do. The scale of work on the estate is increasing every year. In 1938, about 3,000 acres were planted and this year's planting, which is now in full swing, shows an increase of another 1,000 acres. Half of the eight men, who are about to settle on the estate, are miners and the others are labourers. They come from such towns as Blaydon, Stanley and Shiremoor, and, in most cases, have never moved before in their lives."

THE WAR YEARS 1939-1945

The Second World War did not stop further expansion in the Kielder workforce taking place. On 15th September 1939, the Newcastle Journal carried an advertisement for foresters at Kielder: six married couples who would live in their own houses with a rent of three shillings a week and five single men to live in Kielder Bothy. Their wages would be 38 shillings a week minimum and up to 55 shillings a week piece work. It seems that the houses at Castle Drive had formed the nucleus of the new village at Kielder when, on 6th March 1941, the Southern Reporter carried an advertisement for one Bricklayer-Handyman and one Carpenter for the Kielder Estate. A permanent job was available for suitable men, together with houses at four shillings per week exclusive.

It is impossible to appreciate the vital part that timber played in the War Effort. Timber was required in all aspects of service and civilian life. On 21st April 1940, under the headline "Forests of North are Fighting", the Sunday Sun, anxious to stress the importance of forestry, carried the following article: "All around Tyneside, groups of newly-trained men are lying the trees low. The forests of Northumberland are being axed by imported Newfoundland lumberjacks. Women have turned woodsmen and the Lumberjills of the Land Army are at work in the West Cumberland fells. Ex-miners are cutting down woodlands within fifteen miles of Durham and Haltwhistle. Conscientious objectors have been ordered into the forestry service. And through all of Britain's two hundred national forests, by the strange changes of war, unemployed men, who once were desolate in the cities, are now bringing desolation to the larches and firs, the tall pine and spruce, the oak and the chestnut and beech. Wood is a staple war supply.

The Army alone, in the next twelve months, will need a million wooden packing cases for the B.E.F. bacon, ten million timber crates for tinned foods, a million chairs and a million benches, 500,000 wooden beds, 400,000 tables, 40,000,000 feet of timber for lorries, timber for trench supports and timber for railways. And that, of course, merely sets the wooden ball rolling. Wood is a high explosive. As cellulose, it becomes guncotton, as guncotton, it is a component of cordite. As acetone, it produces chloroform, and as cellulose acetate, it goes towards safety glass, the dope of aeroplane fabrics and the photo films with which the R.A.F. snapshots Germany. Pulped into paper, wood provides the Bakelite of the pilot's control board, the reinforced papier mâché helmets of the sappers and the leaflets which we let fall over the Reich. Every shell has a paper lining. Alcohol and motor spirit, sugar and cattle fodder, silk and artificial cotton are found in the forest. At the last Timber Research Exhibition, I even saw gas-masks, sausage skins, chocolates and soldiers' uniforms made from wood."

ARRIVAL OF VALDEMARS BLANKENBURGS IN ENGLAND
MAY 1947

Post-War Britain was in a bad state and in need of urgent repair but there were not enough men and women to fill the millions of job vacancies in manufacturing, agriculture and service industries, so recruiting drives were started in the Displaced Persons camps in Germany, organised by the Ministry of Labour and National Service.

"Baltic Cygnet" signed up young, single women from the Baltic States to work in hospitals and domestic service. "Westward Ho!" aimed to recruit able-bodied men to work in agriculture, forestry, coal-mining and textile factories. Once they reached the work camps, they could apply for the rest of their families to join them, as long as they also passed medical checks so as not to be a burden on the state. About 26,000 Latvians, Lithuanians and Estonians were recruited by the two schemes, which were set up solely as a practical way of filling the many job vacancies.

With the kind permission of Maija Robinson, the youngest of the three children of Valdemars Blankenburgs, the following details have been taken from the diaries, letters and other sources that the family has carefully preserved. The letters that Valdemars and his wife Elfrida exchanged while they were separated are particularly important because they show how Valdemars succeeded in emerging from the confusion and despair that followed the Allied victory in 1945 and brought his family to start a new life in England. Two of the many hundreds may be found towards the end of this book.

Valdemars decided to apply under the 'Westward Ho!' scheme even though it meant leaving his wife with three young children by herself to manage as best she could, while he had to face a solitary existence in a foreign country, not knowing where he would be sent or what work he would be given.

Valdemars: "And so, in the middle of May 1947, I climbed into a truck with a number of other Latvians, leaving my wife and children in a semi-starving Germany to start my journey to an unknown destination in England."

The recruits were first transported to Münster and then to Seedorf transit camp, where they had to undergo medical and security checks. After about two weeks, Valdemars was told to pack his belongings for transport to Cuxhaven, where a ship would be waiting to take them to Hull. He handed his box, which contained most of his clothes, footwear, photographic equipment, tools and his bicycle, over to the camp authorities to load on to the ship and carried only a change of clothes and his valuables, documents, camera etc. in a suitcase that he himself had made out of plywood.

FULL SUTTON They reached the port of Hull late at night and disembarked the following day. Now classed as European Voluntary Workers rather than Displaced Persons, they were taken through Customs and were amazed that their hand luggage was not given even a cursory glance. They loaded their boxes in a truck, climbed into a double-decker bus and were driven to a transit camp on the outskirts of Hull. Next day they continued their journey to the camp at Full Sutton, 15 km. east of York.

First impressions of England were favourable, both regarding food, weather, landscape and people. Valdemars had been expecting the fog, smog, rain, miles of built up suburbs and factory buildings belching smoke that he had been warned about but instead found a pleasant rural landscape, rich in trees and animal life. The weather was sunny and warm, with no rain for weeks. The food was of high quality but the portions were too small for men who had been half-starved in Germany. They were given pocket money with which they bought extra bread and potatoes.

Valdemars was still in the camp at Full Sutton when he heard that there would be a Forestry Commission stand at a forthcoming agricultural show in Lincoln. He determined to go, gain some advice and perhaps make new contacts, even though his English was poor and he had no idea how he would be able to afford the train fare. Being broke, however, is not the same as being broken, and Valdemars was ever an optimist.

At the Lincoln Show, he made contact with the Group Secretary of the English and Welsh Forestry Union, who gave him some useful addresses. He enrolled the help of a Latvian colleague's daughter, who had studied English, and wrote a letter to the Forestry Commission urging them to employ the qualified, experienced foresters from Latvia, since they had found trouble in filling the present job vacancies.

RAWMARSH At the beginning of July, Valdemars was taken with about 100 other Latvians to an agricultural work camp at Rawmarsh near Rotherham. Its official name was "YMCA Hostel" but it had been a German prisoner of war camp. They were all shocked by what awaited them: a complete contrast to their rural surroundings at Full Sutton, where Valdemars had been so delighted with the birds, animals and trees.

"All round we saw factory chimneys. Our new camp was on a bare hillside, old Nissen huts, some wooden. About ½ km. away across the valley were huge clouds of smoke so it was hard to see Rotherham two km. away. Most of us found it hard to breathe."

The Latvian voluntary workers were now in the "Black Country" and could clearly see why it got that name: all the buildings were black, the faces of factory workers going home were black, and they noted that washing had to be dried indoors, otherwise it too would have turned black with soot. The barracks were furnished for 28 men in each with none of the comforts they had been provided with at Full Sutton. No tables, chairs or cupboards. Just rows of two-tier bunks.

Early every morning at Rawmarsh, trucks would pick up the workers from the camp and take them to the local farms. For the next five months, Valdemars hoed fields of potatoes and beet, cleared ditches, harvested corn, picked peas and lifted potatoes. From his wages he had to pay for board and lodging but there was enough left over to send parcels of food and clothing to his family in Germany.

"From our barracks we could see at least a dozen smoking factory chimneys and, when the wind blew from that direction, the air was heavy and sulphur-laden, making breathing difficult. The unaccustomed work of picking potatoes resulted in severe

backache and, during the corn threshing, the dust affected my lungs so badly that I had to seek medical help."

In his spare time, Valdemars built the equipment he needed for developing films and enlarging photographs. He had brought his camera with him and persuaded the camp administration to let him use a spare room as a photographic darkroom. Soon the orders started arriving from the other workers and he was able to earn some extra money. He used most of it to send food parcels to his family in Germany where food rations were becoming more and more unreliable. He also was able to earn a little extra money by mending radios for his colleagues in his spare time.

Things began to change in August 1947 when Valdemars received a letter from a private forest offering him a job as an ordinary worker in a remote area of Scotland. He held back, however, as his goal was to work for the Forestry Commission in his chosen profession of surveyor.

INTERVIEW AT YORK For several weeks Valdemars heard nothing. Finally, at the end of November, he was asked to attend an interview at the Headquarters of the Forestry Commission in York. Forestry in Britain was about to expand on a grand scale, with plans for Kielder Forest to become the largest man-made forest in Europe. Warfare, once again, had made great demands for timber and the task of replanting forests throughout the UK was urgent. The problem for the Forestry Commission was that none of their employees had the skills or experience to draw up maps or blueprints to organise such an expansion that was scheduled to start in the spring of 1948. The War had delayed surveys of those areas of the North Tyne and Upper Redesdale suitable for planting.

Valdemars was questioned by several Forestry Commission officers about projecting roads. *"Because of my poor English, I scarcely understood half the questions, and I imagine they understood even fewer of my replies."* He was handed a plan of a forest and asked to mark a new road between two points. He did his best but was not at all sure that he had passed the test as he was used to working in metres rather than feet and yards and worried about it all the way back to Rawmarsh camp. He was therefore delighted to hear, about a week later, that he was to start work with the Forestry Commission as a surveyor, although he would be paid as an ordinary labourer.

On Friday 5th December 1947, after he got back from work, he received his travel voucher with the order to report to Kielder, his new workplace, on the following Monday. He had to work half-day on Saturday morning and all the offices and shops were shut on Saturday afternoon and Sunday, so he was unable to send the parcels he had promised, or make arrangements for his heavy luggage to be sent by train to Kielder. He entrusted that to his colleagues to arrange, taking only his bike and what he could carry in his Norwegian haversack.

The long awaited offer of work in his chosen profession of forestry meant that he was able to give up the back-breaking work in smoky Rawmarsh and move to the sort of area he was yearning for – quiet, far from industry and, above all, rich in wildlife.

JOURNEY TO KIELDER The journey by rail from Rawmarsh to Kielder was about 200 miles and entailed four changes of train.

"I arrived at Kielder in the dark and was met by a forestry worker with a car, who took me to the hostel where I was to live. There were several young men there, working in forestry, and they were very kind and helpful, which was fortunate, as I had arrived with very little, and my spare clothes and footwear would not arrive for several weeks."

Valdemars would have found this another culture shock but this time a welcome one, to leave the smoke-filled areas of industry one day and wake up the next in a forested area, filling his lungs with pure air once again. He was taken by the District Officer on a tour of the area where he would spend the rest of his working life.

"It soon became clear that the duties of a surveyor were not just surveying; I was expected to do a lot more, such as drawing up compartment boundaries and projecting new roads. In fact, the duties were really those of a road engineer. Although I had experience of similar work in Latvia, the conditions in England were very different, and the problems required a different approach. None of the local workers, including the District Officer, had any experience or knowledge about the planning of afforestation, or the roads or compartment boundaries which would be required."

He could find no manuals setting out the procedures for these tasks and the surveying tools that he received had been obsolete in Latvian forestry practice for many years.

Even the measuring chain he was given did not measure accurately, so he constantly had to subtract 3% when marking the distances on the plans he was given to work with.

"I soon realised that the standard of surveying of the existing plans had been poor and many of the lines seemed to have been drawn in by guesswork. It was on these rather unreliable plans that future surveying had to be based. To make matters even worse, it was winter, the whole area was hilly and by the spring I had to complete the surveying of about 6,000 acres of hill pasture, ready for afforestation. I had little help or advice from the forestry administration and was thus forced to act entirely on my own initiative."

In a letter to his wife, Valdemars described how he coped with the British weather while surveying on the windswept hills in winter:

"I wear my ex-Air Force coat. On the hills, there is a constant strong wind and often rain so it's worth its weight in gold! I can walk all day in the rain and still be completely dry. The thick lining keeps me warm as the imitation leather is windproof. On top of my boots I wear the rubber leggings you made for me for my wild-life photography. Dressed like this, I can walk through rain and long wet grass and still be dry at the end of the day!"

One reminder of Latvia turned out to be Kielder Castle, which was built as a Shooting Lodge for the Duke of Northumberland and dated from 1775. Valdemars discovered that his workplace had been built with timber beams brought by ship from Riga, capital of Latvia, and so the timber for this building had come from the forests of his homeland.

Valdemars threw himself into his work and was given free rein to get on with the job of surveying as he saw fit as his boss had very little idea of what was needed. He set about the task of drawing up new accurate plans of Kielder Forest to show parish boundaries, existing and projected roads, rivers, fire rendezvous points, ancient native forests, geology, etc. The main priority, however, was to overcome bureaucracy and do what was necessary for his family to join him. He knew that families would not get permission to travel until accommodation had been secured so he tried to find something himself with the help of his assistant, a young ex-RAF pilot who knew the area well.

He got on well with the other workers in the Bothy, who helped him out while he awaited the arrival of his luggage, including his photographic equipment, tools, books, clothes and footwear. During all that time, he had to manage with only what he had been able to carry on the train from Rawmarsh. He spent the Christmas of 1947 at the Polish camp near Kielder where there were also two Latvians. The Polish cook shared his interest in photography and so he was well fed. He was also invited to come to the camp when he needed electricity for his photographic work as twenty of the camp inmates had already placed orders for prints. In addition, his work was going well: his surveying had been scrutinised and no faults were found. He was enjoying the peace and quiet of Kielder and earning some extra money with his photography.

"I would like to mention here the great kindness shown to me by the forestry trainees with whom I was living. We had become friends and I had told them about my wife and children in Germany and the shortages of food they were experiencing."

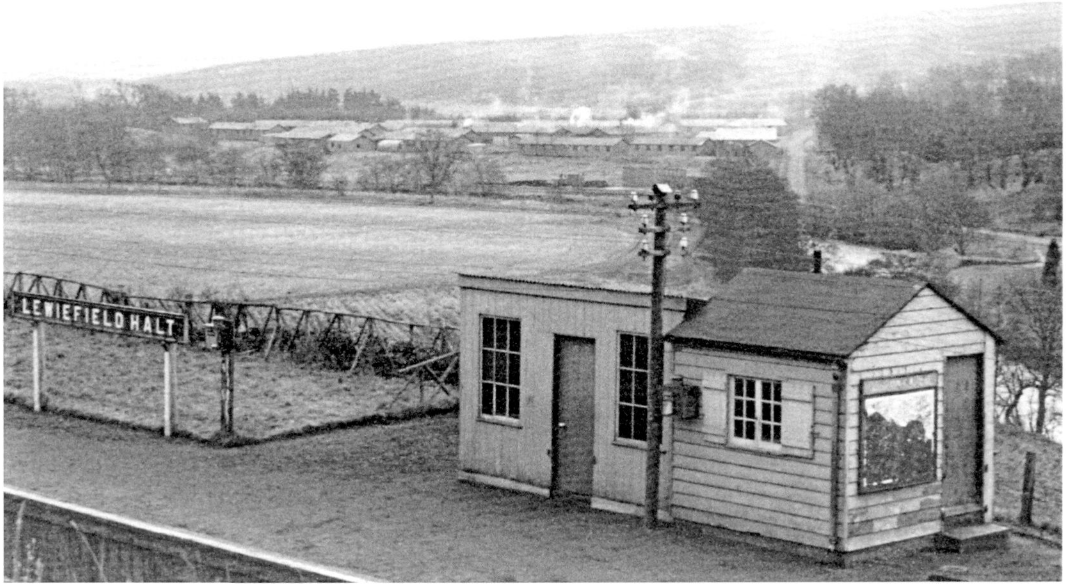

Lewiefield Halt opened in 1933 to serve the newly-built Lewie Camp (later called Kielder Camp) which can be seen in the background. It had been built to house the long-term unemployed as they enrolled on a 12-week rehabilitation course. After the Second World War, it was used to house Displaced Persons who had fled war-torn Europe, including numbers of Poles and Latvians who were given employment in expanding Kielder Forest.

LIVING AT SAUGHTREE 1948-1951

Valdemars had been provided with accommodation in the Bothy at Kielder, where other foresters were lodging, but he urgently needed to find accommodation for his family, if they were to join him. There was nothing available at Kielder for a wife and three young children. His search was at first unsuccessful as any kind of housing in post-war Britain was in short supply. His ex-RAF colleague, however, had located Burnmouth, a small farm cottage at Saughtree, ten miles from Kielder, just over the border in Scotland, which the farmer was willing to rent. He had even cycled there after work, in the dark and rain, to speak to the farmer, who was a friend of his, and got him to write a letter in an attempt to try and speed up the transport application.

Saughtree was a hamlet consisting of a few farms and cottages, a church, a school and a railway station. Immediately, Valdemars rented the cottage and set about spending what little free time he had at weekends on locating furniture (second-hand, as it was cheaper and no coupons were needed) for the new home and digging the garden so that his wife Elfrida could sow the flower seeds she had collected in Germany. With suitable accommodation found, the application for his family to join him progressed with little delay. The year 1948 would prove a good one for Valdemars and his family.

On 12th January 1948, his luggage finally arrived from Rawmarsh camp but, more importantly, it was in the spring that the family were reunited. On 23rd March 1948, Elfrida, his wife, and their three children, Gunis, Dzintra and Maija, landed at Harwich after a night crossing from the Hook of Holland. Identity Cards were stamped and the family was permitted to land. The journey from Harwich to Kielder was not without incident, however, as their escort delivered them to the wrong place, confusing Newcastle (for the train to Kielder) and Newcastleton. The family and their escort arrived at a deserted Newcastleton station to find no Valdemars, who was working and lodging in a remote area of Upper Redesdale, about 10 miles north of Kielder, and knew nothing about their arrival. Some quick phone calls were made by the station master and a forester came out to drive the family to Kielder, where they spent the night in the Bothy to await their family reunion. As Valdemars later recalled:

"I received a telephone call, with the happy news that my family had arrived in Kielder, and that I was to return at once. It was scarcely light next morning when I set off on foot to return to Kielder. I lost my way in the thick mist, as it was the first time I had taken this route. I was not following a road, merely walking in a straight line to Kielder, over heather and rocks. I got lost and so did not reach Kielder until the afternoon."

They were all overjoyed to be together again at last and, although conditions at Burnmouth Cottage were not perfect, it was better than being in Germany. It was their first proper family home after four years in various Displaced Persons camps. The manager of the hostel at Kielder had helped Valdemars to buy some second-hand furniture in Newcastle: a table, one bed and four chairs. There were no modern conveniences in Burnmouth: no electricity, no central heating, cooker, fridge, washing machine, water heater, vacuum cleaner or any of the other things that are now taken for granted. There was only one bedroom which the two sisters shared with their parents while their elder brother slept in an alcove off the kitchen. On their first night at Burnmouth, the family had slept partly on the floor, with a few blankets because their main luggage, including clothes and household items, had not arrived from London. And it never did. Somehow, most of the things that the family had brought with them from Latvia and Germany had got lost in transit. The family had to make do with candles until Valdemars was able to buy an oil lamp. In the midge season, however, they had to shut all the windows before the lamp was lit, otherwise the room would be filled with swarms of insects, all hungry for blood.

"We had no coal or any other fuel to use for heating or cooking. To get coal, you had to get a special permit from the coal depot several miles away. I could not stay for long with my family, as I had to get back to work in Redesdale, so I had to leave my wife on her own to sort out all the problems as best she could, with her limited English."

Their landlord, Mr. Paterson, who lived at Burnmouth Farm, was very kind and brought them a paraffin stove as the open range, heated by coal, was old and inefficient. Since the cottage had neither a bath nor hot water and the farm had both, Mr. Paterson let the whole family have a bath on Saturdays. The weekly rent of 3/6 (3 shillings and 6 pence) included permission to collect brushwood from the forest and the use of a horse and cart to transport it, as well as for fetching coal from the depot. All the family's washing had to be done either by hand in the sink or in the boiler where the water was heated by a coal fire underneath.

Most items of food, clothing and other goods were still rationed and they had no ration books. Elfrida was able to buy some un-rationed items from the grocery van when it stopped at the cottage. When she asked for milk for the children, however, the grocer explained that, unfortunately, milk was on the ration and apologised for not being able to sell her any. But later, on his return journey, he knocked on the door, and handed her two bottles of milk with the words "For your children." On another occasion, he gave them a cake, which was a great treat. To obtain ration books they had to go to the Police Station in Hawick, which was about 20 miles away, and the only way to get there was by train. The nearest station was Riccarton Junction which had no road access. This meant a trek of about two miles, first through the grass and heather up one side of Saughtree Fell and then over the gravel on the sides of the railway sleepers until they got to the railway station. Then they had to find out how to buy train tickets, where to get the train to Hawick, find the Police Station, explain what they needed in an unfamiliar language and then make their way back again to Burnmouth Cottage.

Once the family had secured ration books, they were able to get some supplies from the Carruthers and Scott grocery van from Newcastleton. The children were fascinated, marvelling at the novelty of a food shop that travelled on wheels. Mr. Scott, the owner and driver, sat on a stool inside, noting every item in his duplicate pad with its piece of carbon paper. The van had wooden shelving, stacked with unfamiliar foodstuffs which Mr. Scott tried to explain as they crowded round, staring at all the interesting items. The children were given sweet ration coupons which they eagerly used to buy something from the very limited choice on offer, often just sticks of liquorice root or "Victory V" lozenges, neither of which could be described as sweets. A butcher and a fishmonger would also call on different days so they always had to be on the lookout for the next food delivery. The family started to relax and enjoy the warm weather, though Elfrida was anxious about how they would manage. She was also worried about Valdemars wearing himself out, having to walk all day in the hills in all weathers, on top of which he had a gruelling cycle ride to and from Kielder.

Getting to a main town to buy necessities, visit the dentist or optician meant catching the train to Hawick. This again entailed an expedition of climbing up Saughtree Fell, usually through wet grass to reach the railway line, where they left their wellies in the platelayers' hut to change into town shoes to walk along the railway line to Riccarton Junction, a small isolated hamlet. Most of the residents worked for the railway. As there was no road access, it had its own school, post office and grocery shop. There was a Refreshment Room on the platform where tea, sandwiches and cake were sold while passengers waited for their train.

Another challenge for the Blankenburgs family was learning the language. Valdemars picked it up quickly as he had to use it daily with his colleagues, though he was sometimes defeated by the broader dialects. But getting to work and back was proving harder than he had anticipated:

"Every morning and evening, I had to cycle a distance of about 6 miles, often in rain and strong winds. My work entailed walking in steep, hilly country. I was so tired when I got

home that I had to go to bed straight after my meal. All my efforts to find accommodation nearer Kielder were in vain and I just had to put up with the situation."

The loss of their luggage was extremely distressing but there was some consolation. Valdemars told his colleagues at Kielder about it and they arranged a request for compensation, but this involved several trips to Hawick to give particulars. In January 1949, however, the family received £60 in compensation, with which Valdemars was able to buy a second-hand Royal Enfield motorcycle. That did not happen until after Christmas 1950, however, so he had to keep cycling in all the wild weather that was thrown at Saughtree with its rain, snow, ice and gales.

Mr Paterson, their landlord, was a widower and, when his housekeeper left, he offered the post to Elfrida. She agreed to work seven days a week from 9.00 a.m. to 3.00 p.m. cooking and cleaning. For that she was given £1 a week cash, plus free milk and potatoes, which the children collected from the farm. The job at the farm entailed a lot of cleaning and scrubbing which had to be done by hand. There were no rubber gloves available until the 1950s, nor gentle cleaning materials, and so her hands became very chapped and sore from the harsh carbolic soap. Sometimes her skin cracked and bled.

They tried to be as self-sufficient as possible and grew potatoes, cabbages and other vegetables. The cabbage was finely shredded, salt and caraway seeds were added before it was packed in a large crock to ferment into sauerkraut, providing the family with vitamins as well as a taste of Latvian cuisine. They also carried on the continental tradition of foraging for forest mushrooms in the autumn. This raised some eyebrows as the locals were convinced that they were all poisonous. They also picked wild fruits such as blackberries, blueberries, rowan berries, which made delicious bitter-sweet preserves, and juicy golden raspberries, which grew near the house. Other finds included hazel nuts, crab apples and rosehips.

If Valdemars had relied on the Forestry Commission to find accommodation, as they had originally promised, the family would not have got out of Germany for another three years, as it was only in 1951 that they finally got round to it when Valdemars gave the Forestry Commission an ultimatum: either find him decent family accommodation at Kielder and pay him a surveyor's wage or he would resign and seek work elsewhere, possibly abroad. This came about after Valdemars suffered a serious motorcycle accident, while going home in the dark during a snowstorm. He gashed his leg quite badly and it was agreed that he couldn't carry on like that. His boss was shocked as he had come to rely on him. He agreed to pay him the proper wage and also advised Valdemars to apply for British citizenship so that his children would eventually be able to get free university education. Citizenship was granted on 15th September 1954.

Suitable accommodation soon became available and Kielder became their next home. It was the Castle Bungalow, a wooden building which had been used as a hostel for forestry trainees. This offer of accommodation was gladly accepted as Valdemars would no longer have to travel those punishing miles to and from work. Castle Bungalow was only a few minutes' walk to his office in Kielder Castle. The bungalow did not have electricity but it did have a proper bathroom, complete with a bath and hot water. There were four bedrooms so the family could let out one bedroom to a boarder for some extra income. A Latvian draughtsman, who worked with Valdemars and found life in Kielder Camp unsatisfactory, became their lodger. Valdemars would still spend his day walking in the hills carrying out his surveying tasks but would at least be spared the twice-daily motor-bike journeys from Saughtree in often inclement weather. They still had some of the things that they had brought from Latvia and Germany, except for those items which were lost by the railway company, and they had also acquired some furniture, crockery and other household goods. As Elfrida remarked:

"We packed our belongings once again, ready for the move across the Border: So ended the first stage of our life on British soil. In the spring of 1951, we moved to Kielder."

For the next 20 years, Kielder would be home for Valdemars Blankenburgs where he could enjoy his three passions: family, forestry and photography. His devotion to his growing family, including five grandchildren, and forestry goes without saying and volumes could be written about the photographic archive of over 10,000 pictures that he built up. He had been unable to bring all his early photographs as he and his family fled war-torn Europe but he managed to bring some of his favourites, which were stored in the pram of Maija, the youngest of his three children.

The Blankenburgs family lived at Kielder, first at Castle Bungalow and then in the new Forestry Village at Butteryhaugh. It was formally opened by Lord Robinson, chairman of the Forestry Commission on 27th May 1952, though building continued for several years after that and included a large new school to cater for the planned influx of new foresters and their families. Life was good in Butteryhaugh, though the new labour force of 2,000 foresters did not materialise as machinery took over from men.

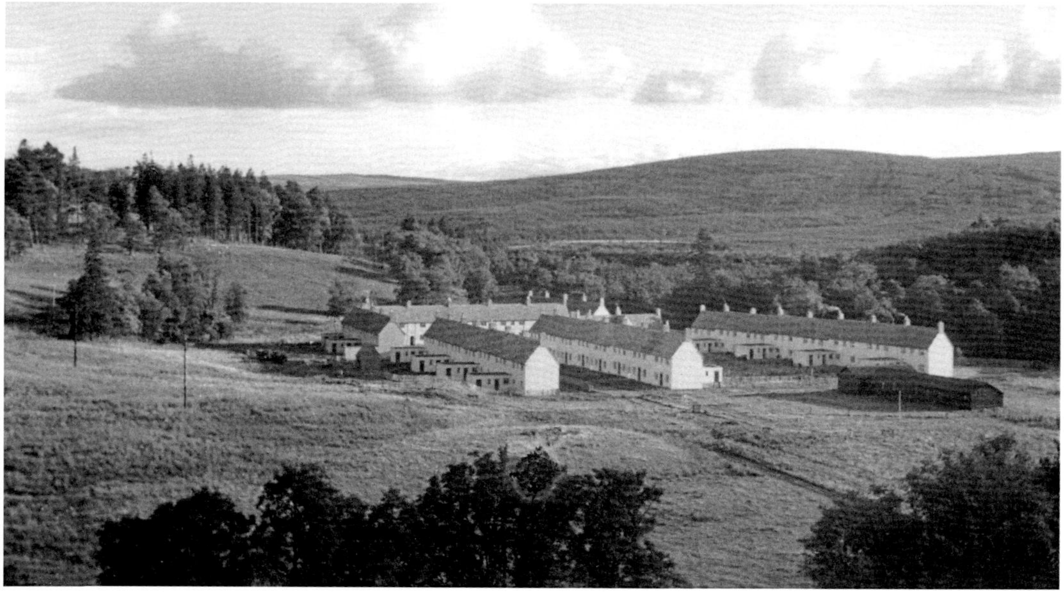

The new Forestry village of Butteryhaugh c.1953

THE COTTAGE RETREAT AT BELLINGBURN HEAD

Kielder would be remote enough for most people, especially after the closure of the railway in 1956, but not remote enough for Valdemars Blankenburgs. In 1961, a unique opportunity arose for Valdemars to go to a higher level of isolation when, for £12 a year, he rented from the Forestry Commission the cottage of Bellingburn Head, high up the Belling Burn, beyond the original Plashetts drift coal mine and houses known as Seldom Seen. He made this cottage, which had once been the shepherd's cottage for The Belling, very much a retreat for himself and his family where he could photograph wildlife and enjoy the isolation of the hills. It became the place where his heart and amazing energies were engaged.

The following account is taken from a newspaper article that was written in 1973 as plans for Kielder Reservoir were being discussed. A journalist, accompanied by a professional photographer who took the portrait photograph below, interviewed Valdemars in Bellingham. Afterwards they were driven by him to Bellingburn Head.

"As we drive along one of the 500 miles of muddy Forestry roads that he planned, surveyed and walked, every turn is familiar, every plantation known.

"This is an old pele, one of the fortified stone houses, in which families and animals took refuge from Border Reivers. This corner is where the water will reach if Kielder Reservoir comes – all these little trees will have to be removed and destroyed. You see this canvas

hut. It is a hide for me because deer often come to this place. And that hide in the middle of the field is where you see the blackcock lekking. These are the displays and often the fights of the male blackcock in the mating season. But I must get inside by about 4.30 in the morning. There is not enough light for filming until around seven and so I just sit and listen to the sounds outside."

It is too wet to take the car further, so we set off in gumboots alongside a rushing stream rusty with peat water. Two or three footbridges have been swept away in torrential springs – and so was the water-powered generator that he rigged up beside the waterfalls on the other side of Belling Burn Head. We leap along the marshy path to rocks beside a thundering, angry force. Dizzily, I peer at the remains of the wooden channel and pipes. The wires still reach up the bank. This indefatigable man paused:

"I think I will have another try one day. And here is my pond I dug out. I had about 150 little trout but I do not know if they have got through the winter. And this bit of land with the new trees I got from the Commission when they wanted to put the rent up. I told them no flowers grew in my garden because of the wind so I needed more land. This is a hedge of Norwegian spruce – it will last about 50 years. I have 40 different species of trees. Some came from Latvia in envelopes, as tiny seeds."

Fruit trees are lovingly staked along the walls – blackberries, with extra shelter, raspberry canes, gooseberries, plums. And always his wife's flowers and conversation alive with the knowledge and awareness of the history of this land that is now theirs."

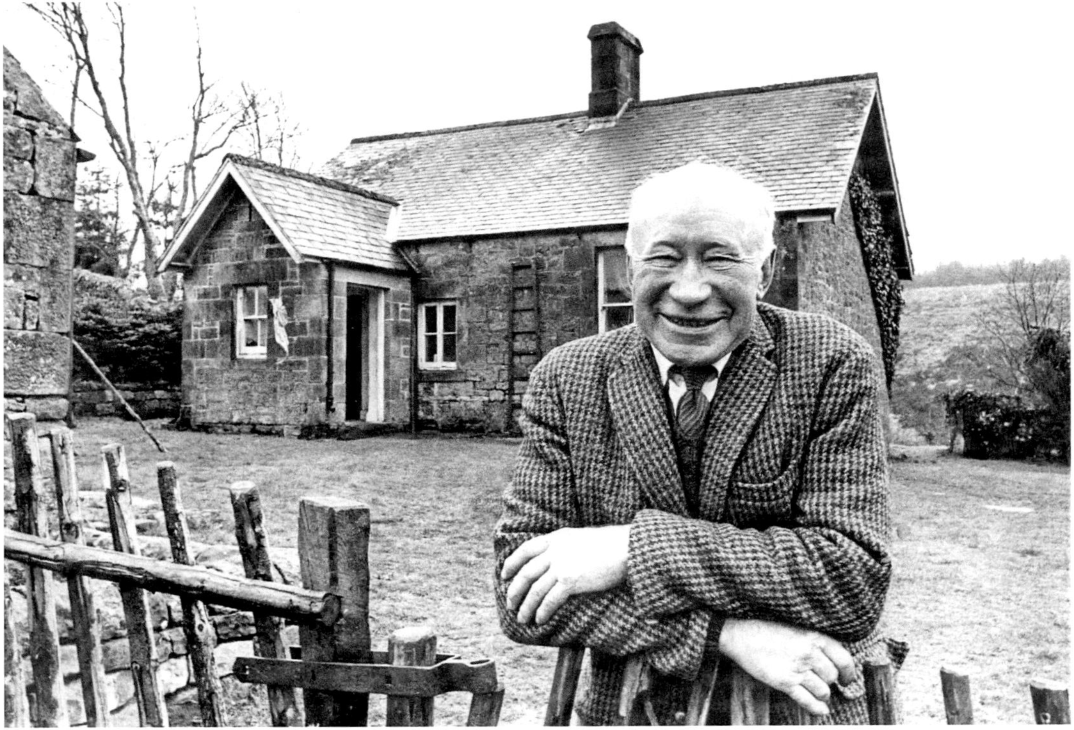

A Picture of Contentment

Valdemars Blankenburgs outside his cottage at Bellingburn Head

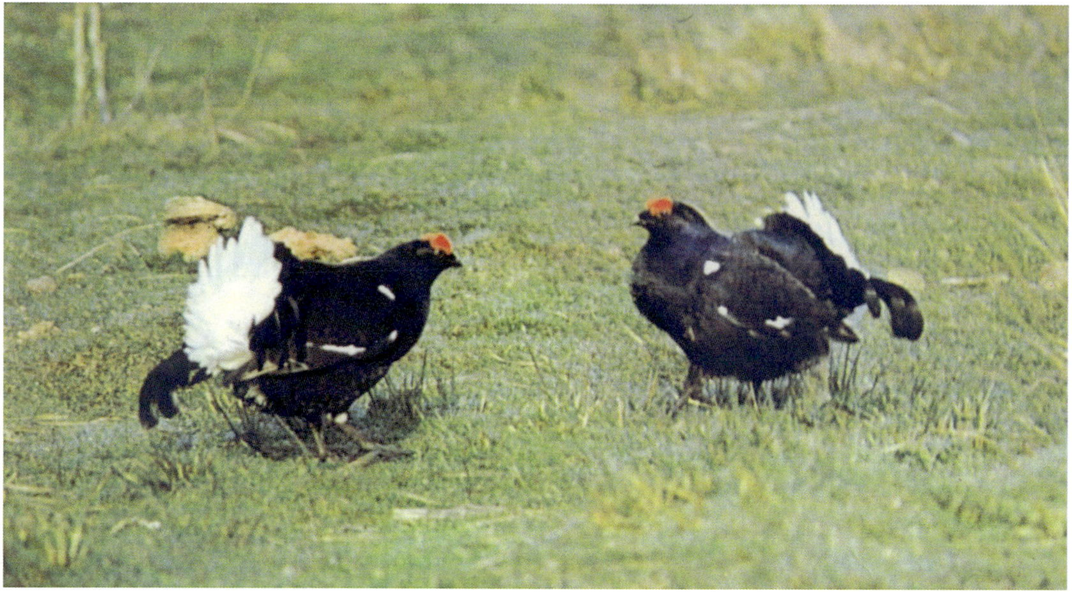

Valdemars Blankenburgs was a dedicated and patient photographer of wild life and he built a hide at Bellingburn Head to photograph the lekking of the Black Cock. "These are the displays and often the fights of the male blackcock in the mating season. But I must get inside the hide by about 4.30 in the morning. There is not enough light for filming until around seven and so I just sit and listen to the sounds outside." This photograph was later produced as a postcard.

THE BLANKENBURGS LEGACY 1947-1991

Over the following years, until he retired on 26th February 1971, Valdemars Blankenburgs fulfilled his duties to the Forestry Commission, finally becoming Clerk of Works and based in his office in Kielder Castle. In addition to his normal duties, he was building up a unique collection of photographs recording every aspect of Kielder Forest, which would become part of the Blankenburgs Legacy. For the last 20 years of his life, Valdemars and Elfrida retired to Cairns Road in Bellingham.

Their house looked out across the disused railway line, which had closed to passengers in 1956. Upon their arrival at their new home, the first thing that Valdemars did was to plant trees – lodge pole pines, broom, Norwegian pine, spruce and willow. Even on a bleak April day, the garden displayed his wife's favourite flowers – primula, forsythia, daffodils and the last of the Christmas roses. As important as the garden, however, was the darkroom where Valdemars continued to do his photography. Shelves all around held developing paper, trays, chemicals and boxes lettered, of course, in Latvian. There was barely room to slip into the kitchen chair, in front of which was his enlarger.

"I push my wife's clothes out of the cupboard in the bedroom. I fit a little heater at floor level and a fan in the roof so as to have air. Everything I need is here."

In addition to his photography, which would become an increasingly important feature of his retirement, he played a major part in the life of Bellingham as a member of the

Parish Council. One of his actions concerned the state of a village phone box, which judges had criticised in a recent best-kept village competition. He devised a simple experiment to test the claims of the post office, who were then responsible for cleaning telephone boxes, that they were cleaned once a week. He found an empty match box in one of the phone boxes and, after discreetly dating it, found that the same match box was still there a month later. This was duly sent to the head post office for comment and was reported in the Journal under the heading "Post Office told to come clean" on 28th December 1973.

He was a founder member of the Bellingham & North Tyne local history group, which flourished between 1967 and 1992 and visited Bellingburn Head in May 1981. He also joined the camera club and the natural history society. Acutely aware of the changes that had taken place in his lifetime and in the countryside, he was determined not to let them pass unrecorded. The result was what is now called the Blankenburgs Legacy.

(1) Tape recordings of local people

With a particular interest in the history of Bellingham and the North Tyne where he had made his home, Valdemars Blankenburgs made recordings of the people that he met in the course of his work and travels around Kielder and the North Tyne Valley. These recordings complemented the Oral History Project then being carried out by the National Park. Of particular interest are the recordings that he made of people like William L. McCavish, head forester, John Hedley of Bewshaugh Farm, Jack Cowan, last tenant of Wellhaugh Farm, or John Proudlock, who had lived and worked at the remote colliery and village of Plashetts, which was connected to Plashetts station by a wagonway and incline. It is thanks to his recordings that we know more about the lives of families of the North Tyne and the colliery village that was gradually abandoned in the 1930s. Recording people was not always easy, however, as Valdemars recalled:

"Some people are frightened of the machine; or they do not want to speak to a stranger; or they make other excuses. Now I write out many of the questions in advance so that they can go over these alone or with a friend and in that way they often remember little things they thought they had forgotten."

(2) Photography of the North Tyne Valley before flooding by Kielder Reservoir.

As proposals materialised to flood part of the North Tyne Valley between Falstone and Kielder to construct Kielder Reservoir in the mid-1970s, he made a photographic study of the houses and farms about to be razed to the ground and submerged forever beneath the waters of Kielder Reservoir along with thousands of trees. Houses from Emmethaugh to Bewshaugh, including Shilburnhaugh, Otterstone Lee, Mounces, The Belling, Law, Plashetts and those along the Whickhope Burn stood ready to be razed to the ground along with the more modern Forestry Commission housing. In addition, thousands of trees were felled to prevent trunks or branches being swept into the dam at Tower Knowe and causing irreparable damage to the two electricity turbines built into the structure of the dam. Photographs taken just before flooding began reveal a deserted, desolate and depressing landscape, reminiscent of the battlefields of the Somme of World War One or the carpet bombing of World War Two.

It is ironic that, while Otterstone Lee was flooded, the little two-room cottage of Leaplish, which housed the shepherd for the farm's Leaplish hirsel, was just elevated enough to escape the waters of the Reservoir. It now stands safely on the shore above the water as a fine example of the shepherds' cottages that once dotted the hills of the North Tyne, Redesdale and Coquetdale where shepherds made a hard-won living.

The pictures in this book are a tiny fraction of the photographs that he took and processed himself in his darkroom. We have concentrated on the buildings that he photographed in the mid-1970s when he had retired but knew that the new Kielder Reservoir would drown them forever. Not that anything of them would remain prior to the flooding which began in late 1978. What would have upset him most would have been the razing to the ground of every building and every tree in the flooding area to prevent any debris being drawn into the two turbines that were buried in the dam wall to generate electricity.

(3) Production of six volumes of archive photographs copied from pictures lent or donated by locals.

Encouraged by the tape recordings that he had made of locals talking about old times, Valdemars switched his attention to visual records, including postcards and family photographs. These provided the impetus for him to extend his photographic legacy by building up a collection of over 1,500 archive photographs of Bellingham and neighbourhood dating from the 1860s. It was the beginning of a remarkable project, which has made a unique contribution to the history of Northumberland.

The Bellingham archive began at a Bellingham Parish Council meeting in 1975 when he pointed out that there were many old photographs of Bellingham and the surrounding area that were liable to be lost or were deteriorating because of the lack of permanency of the old photographic processing methods.

It was agreed that it would be a good idea to preserve these old photographs and, at the same time, place a selection in an album, which people could view in Bellingham library. And it was Councillor Blankenburgs who suggested than an appeal should go out for old photographs to put in the album.

The appeal exceeded all expectations. Instead of a few faded snapshots, Valdemars was inundated with a steady avalanche of photographs. Towards the end of the appeal, 1,200 photographs had been gathered of all shapes, sizes and conditions, which came in from all corners of the district and even further afield.

It was obvious that there were going to be far too many photographs for a single album so a small committee of local residents was formed to sift through the photographs and select ones suitable for the collection. The committee had already been active in encouraging the villagers to send them in, through individual members of the Parish Council, the Local History Group and the Hexham Courant.

The committee of five local residents, including Valdemars Blankenburgs, managed to reduce the "possibilities" to 502 and then came the long, painstaking process of copying each individual picture, all of which was done by Valdemars himself in his darkroom in Cairns Road.

These photographs were printed and the committee began the selection process again to produce a collection of 274 photographs. Valdemars brought out his enlarger again to print the photographs to go on public display. It was decided to use three albums instead of one and 203 photographs finally made it. These three albums give a better history of Bellingham than any history book.

The pictures were split up into 16 different sections, taking in views and landscapes, buildings, district and parish councils, trades and employment, transport, arts, schools, social life and local people, church and chapel, recreation and entertainment, games and sports, defence and mobilisation, 1918 peace and other celebrations, the 1911 Great Flood, fashions, the Bellingham Show and a miscellaneous section.

The exercise had been a model in community effort for, although the cost on a commercial scale would have been frightening, the actual cost borne by Bellingham Parish Council was no more than £50. The committee spent around 300 working hours selecting photographs and finding out details of each of them. Valdemars spent as many hours copying the original pictures, processing the negatives, making the enlargements and mounting the finished prints in bound photographic albums. All of this was done out of love for the past and free of charge, with only the cost of the materials being charged to the Parish Council.

At a special ceremony on Wednesday 6th October 1976, three albums of photographs were formally handed over to Bellingham library, where a special exhibition was also staged. The delight of the locals was plain to see as they picked out great grannies, forgotten schoolmates and local characters. Enlargements of some of the photographs were made, some with the original beside them, to show how the photographic skill of Valdemars Blankenburgs had helped to preserve the history that could have been lost forever.

At a second ceremony on Wednesday 10th December 1986, an additional three albums of photographs were handed over to Bellingham library. Valdemars Blankenburgs made a touching speech in which he said that the albums were his way of thanking the North Tyne community:

"When I came here just after the War, the people of Kielder and Bellingham were very helpful and kind to me and my wife and helped us to start a new life from scratch. We have been accepted into the community and I felt that I had to repay you in some small way. Anything I can do for the community I will always be very glad to do."

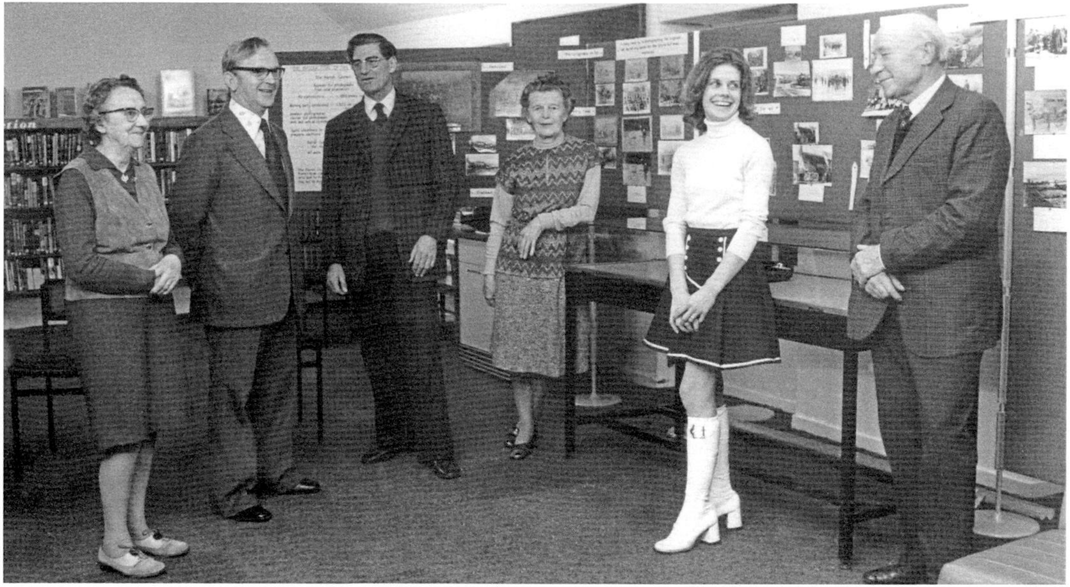

The people who created the Photographic Albums

Pictures & Descriptions: Dorothy Inglis, Graham Robson Batey, William Edwin Lawrence, Jean Milburn

Typing: Patricia Gaskin

Photography: Valdemars Blankenburgs

(4) Transference of his photographic archive to the Forestry Commission and then to Northumberland Archives for safe keeping as a photographic archive.

On Tuesday 11th December 1984, Valdemars Blankenburgs handed over to the Northumberland Country Record Office his archive of over ten thousand photographs showing the changing face of Kielder and the North Tyne Valley since he came to Kielder as a refugee from Latvia in December 1947. The collection also included archive photographs, maps and plans, and taped interviews with residents of the North Tyne Valley and miners from the former Plashetts Colliery before its closure in the 1930s. The material was given on the condition that people would be given ready access to it.

It was remarked that the production of the six albums, which remained in Bellingham, was a fantastic achievement and ensured that the ordinary people of Bellingham and neighbourhood would have a place in history. No other parish had such a detailed record of the life of a community over such a long period.

(5) Scots pines and future reseeding projects

“Were I asked to sketch ‘the end of the world’ I should take my stand at the head of the Kielder or Scaup Burn.” Rambler, Newcastle Daily Journal, 24th January 1914.

About 1955, Valdemars observed and photographed some Scots pines growing on William’s Cleugh, a remote hillside some distance from Kielderhead Farm. His photograph was later reproduced facing page 41 in the Border Forest Park Guide (Walton, 1958). At the time, these pines were believed to be possible survivors of an indigenous forest. Debate followed among foresters, including Valdemars Blankenburgs himself, as to how these Scots pines managed to survive at this point. A descendant of the thousands of Scots pines that once formed the forests of the Borders? Or a wind-borne seed? Or a way marker deliberately planted and tended? The true explanation may perhaps never be known and must remain the subject for academic debate. The upshot, however, has been a determination to reseed this area with native Scots pines as part of a wider programme to create areas where native trees can grow among trees planted and harvested for commercial purposes.

Little did Valdemars Blankenburgs know that his photograph of Scots pines above Kielderhead Farm would lead to a major reseeding project in the 21st century. Between 2018 and 2023, staff and volunteers from the Northumberland Wildlife Trust planted alder, birch, elm and willow, as well as Scots pines, supporting the few existing Scots pines. More than 30,000 trees were planted over 95 hectares to recreate a wild landscape within the boundaries of Kielder Forest. The observation that Valdemars Blankenburgs made in the mid-1950s has been realised some 70 years later.

Kielderhead Wildwood is a partnership project between the Northumberland Wildlife Trust and Forestry England. A full account of the Reseeding project can be found in the book "Reseeding: Restoring wildness at Kielderhead Wildwood" published by the Northumberland Wildlife Trust. Details on the Northumberland Wildlife Trust website.

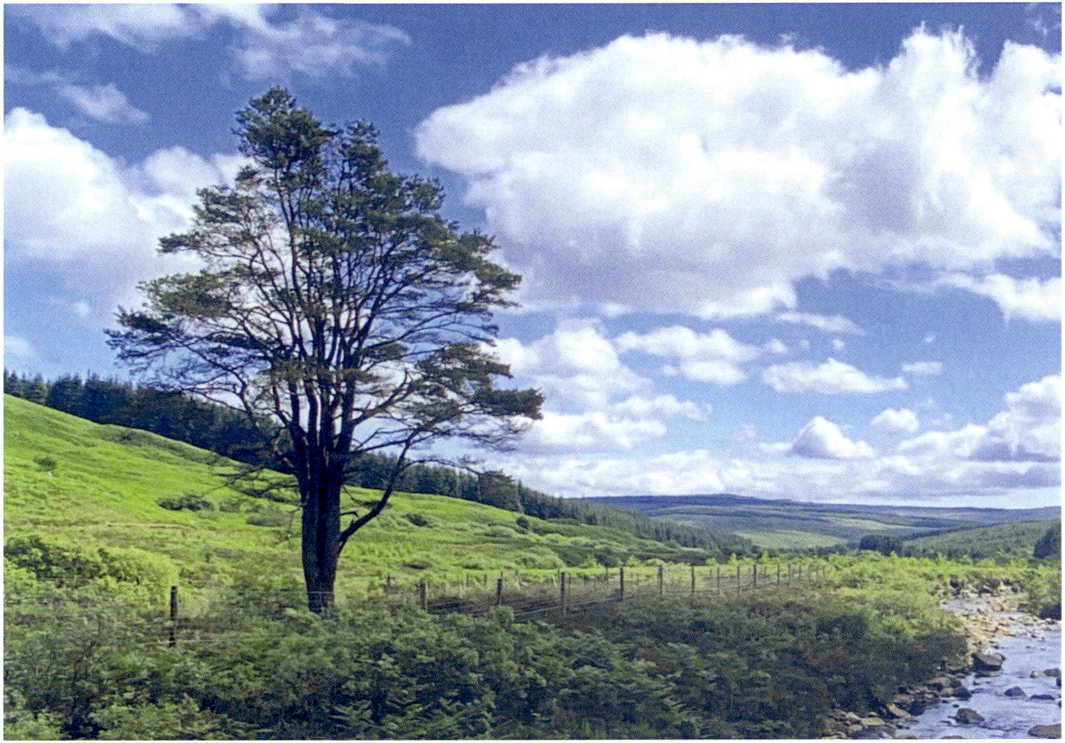

One of the native Scots pines, last relics of the Ancient Pinewoods, in William's Cleugh, up the Scaup Burn, Kielder. (photo: Natasha Hemsley)

During the 44 years that he lived in Kielder and Bellingham, Valdemars Blankenburgs became a well-known figure who would do anything he could for the local community. In addition to his ability to mend radios and televisions, he was often called upon to provide photographs of official and social events. Older residents still treasure the photographs that he took of their wedding day.

His unique archive of over 10,000 photographs and over a dozen taped interviews were finally lodged with the Northumberland Record Office on 11th December 1984. The six albums of local archive photographs remained in Bellingham, firstly in the Library and subsequently in the Heritage Centre.

Valdemars Blankenburgs died at Cairns Road on 18th February 1991. Although he died a few months before Latvia regained her independence, he knew it was imminent. From his arrival in Britain, he had eagerly followed the news from the Baltics on his short-wave radio, with Voice of America broadcasts from Eastern Europe being particularly informative in spite of constant Russian jamming of the airwaves. By 1990, he knew that Latvia would soon be recognised as an independent country so, although he suffered a fatal heart attack so shortly before it became a reality, he died a happy man.

At a service in St. Cuthbert's Church in Bellingham his eldest grandson Andris read Philip Larkin's poem "The Trees" and the Latvian National Anthem was played. His ashes were returned in the following year to the recently independent Latvia and interred in a beautiful forest glade in Courland, his birthplace.

THE PHOTOGRAPHS OF VALDEMARS BLANKENBURGS

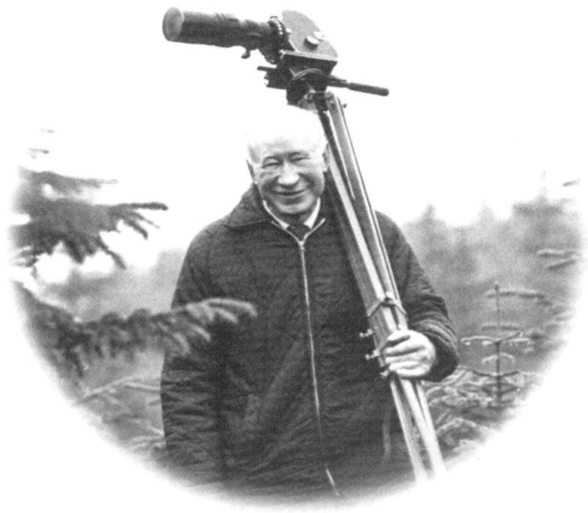

Valdemars Blankenburgs played a large part in Bellingham life when he and Elfrida moved to Cairns Road in 1968, including service as a Bellingham Parish Councillor and a founder member of the local history society. One of his greatest achievements was to create a photographic archive of Bellingham, the North Tyne Valley and Redesdale using contemporary and archive photographs, some borrowed for copying and some of his own. These were mounted in six albums and made freely available to locals and visitors in Bellingham library.

This involved a great deal of organisation and work, especially in the darkroom, as the pictures had to be copied on film and then printed using chemicals. All of this took hundreds of hours of work in the darkroom before digital scanning was known.

The photographs in this book are a tiny percentage of the thousands that he took. Some were printed, some remained as negatives and a few were published as colour postcards.

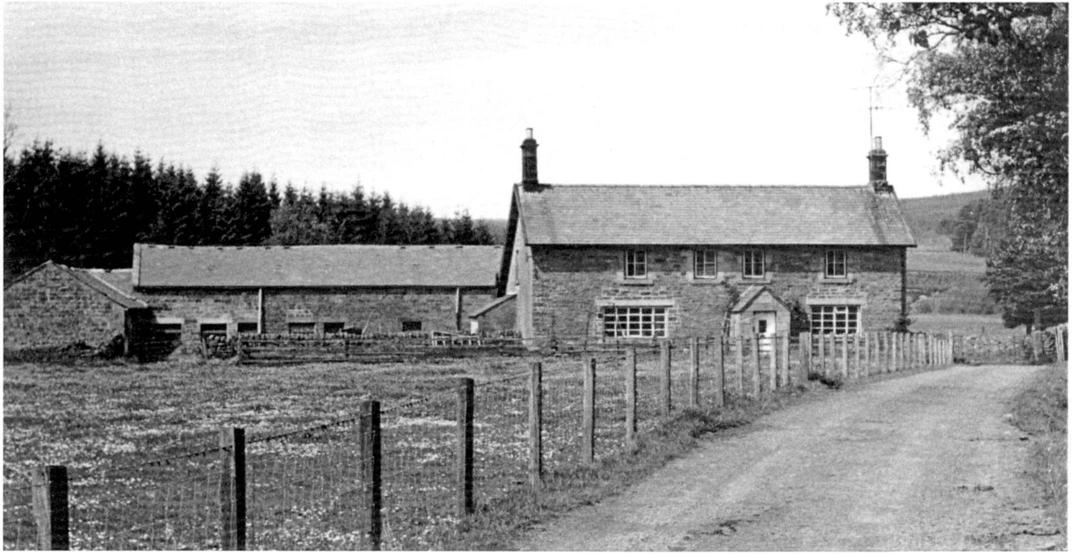

The Lost Houses of the North Tyne

Emmethaugh was a farm of 60 acres and its location at the lower end of the North Tyne Valley made it ideal for dairy farming. On 2nd April 1971, the Newcastle Evening Chronicle carried an article titled "The Valley of the Dammed" in which Mr. Syd Harrison bemoaned the prospect of leaving the farm that he had built up over the previous sixteen years to supply milk to the valley. "I don't know what I will do," he said. "I'll just have to look for a council house somewhere and some kind of job."

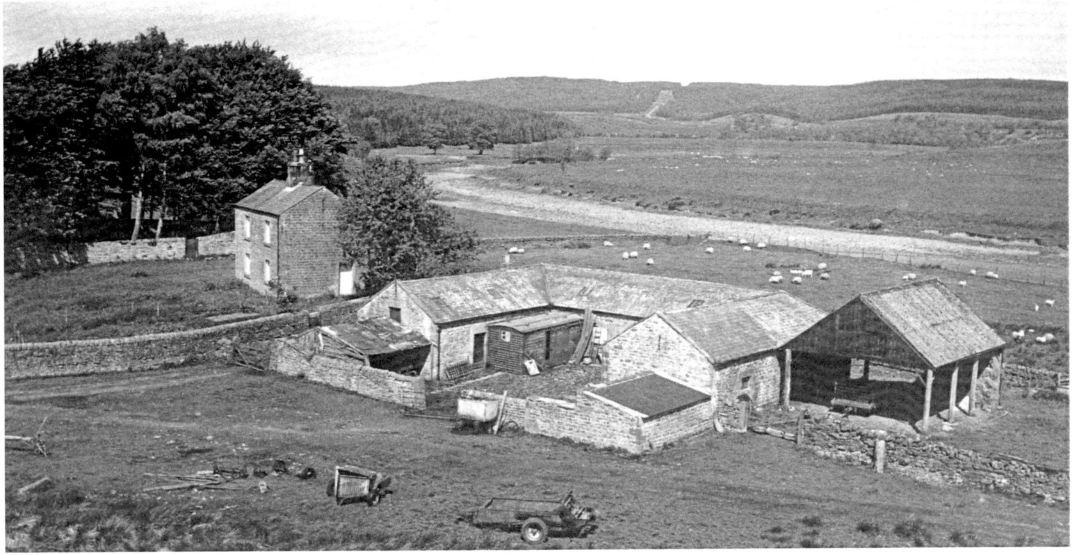

The Lost Houses of the North Tyne

Shilburnhaugh was a hill farm of 565 acres, including 24 acres of inbye pasture, which carried roughly 350 Blackfaced sheep. For a month in the autumn of 1977, residents at Shilburnhaugh won an injunction to stop further work on Kielder Reservoir until they had won guarantees from the Northumbrian Water Authority concerning compensation and their relocation to new semi-detached houses at Hawkhope Hill, Falstone, which, at £35,000 each, were the costliest council houses ever built.

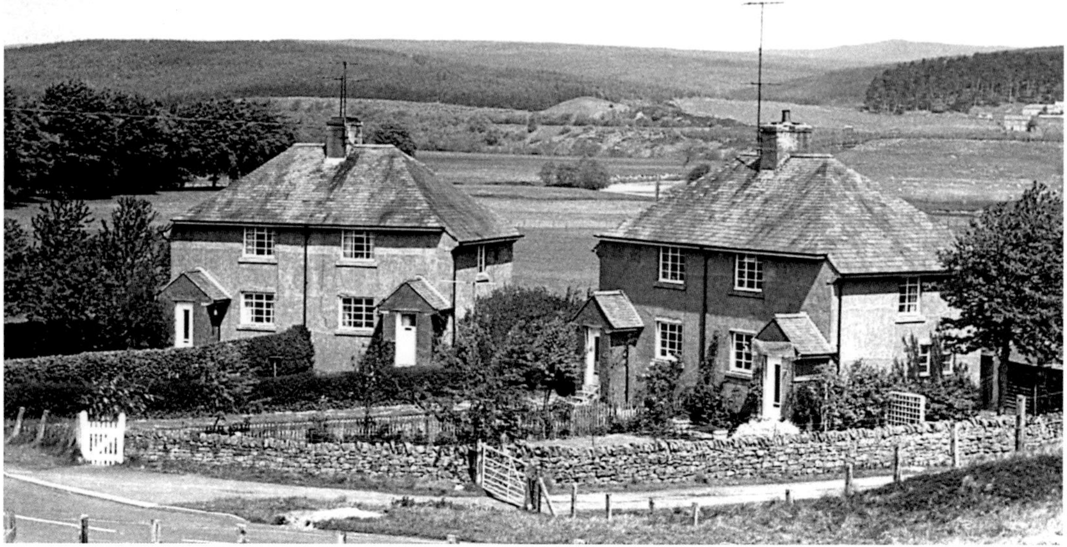

The Lost Houses of the North Tyne

Shilburnhaugh Forestry Commission Houses were examples of the dwellings that the Forestry Commission built from the 1930s as the numbers of men required to plant Kielder Forest increased. They were built near existing farms, as at Emmethaugh, Whickhope, The Forks, Plashetts and Bewshaugh, where ten bungalows were built. The Belling Farm is visible in the top right-hand corner of the photograph behind a pair of Victorian railway platelayers' cottages which overlooked the railway line.

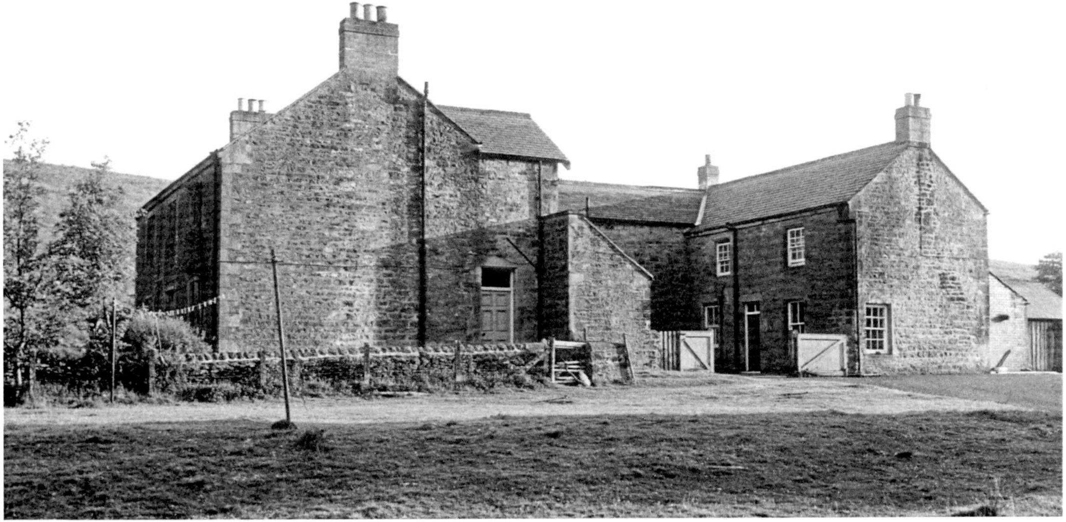

The Lost Houses of the North Tyne

Whickhope Lodge was a favourite haunt of sportsmen before the arrival of Kielder Forest and Kielder Reservoir. The 11,800-acre estate guaranteed good sport and this account in the Hexham Courant of 1906 was typical: Captain Cuthbert and a party of five other sportsmen had very good sport, shooting over the butts on Whickhope, Cranecleugh and Smale farms. They bagged 235 brace on 19th and 20th August and 233½ brace on 29th and 30th, making a total of 468½ brace for the four days' shoot.

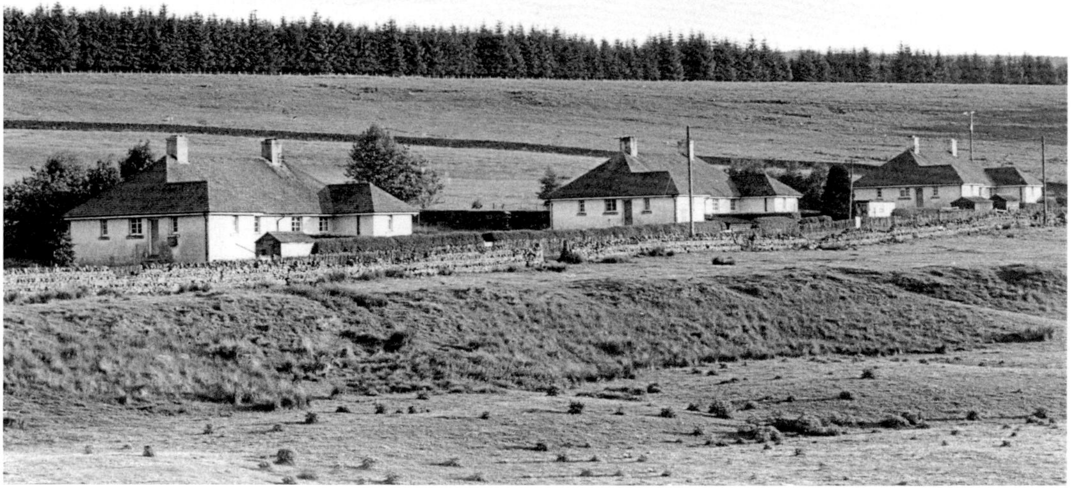

The Lost Houses of the North Tyne

Six Forestry Commission Bungalows were built in the 1930s in the valley of the Whickhope Burn, near the Nissen huts of the former Summer Camp which housed the long-term unemployed on a 10-week rehabilitation course. Some of the Nissen huts were later used by the Forestry Commission as storage sheds. "The nearest shop was in Falstone but hardly anyone at Whickhope had cars so we relied on the mobile shops of local grocers. Every night we walked up to Whickhope Farm to get the milk."

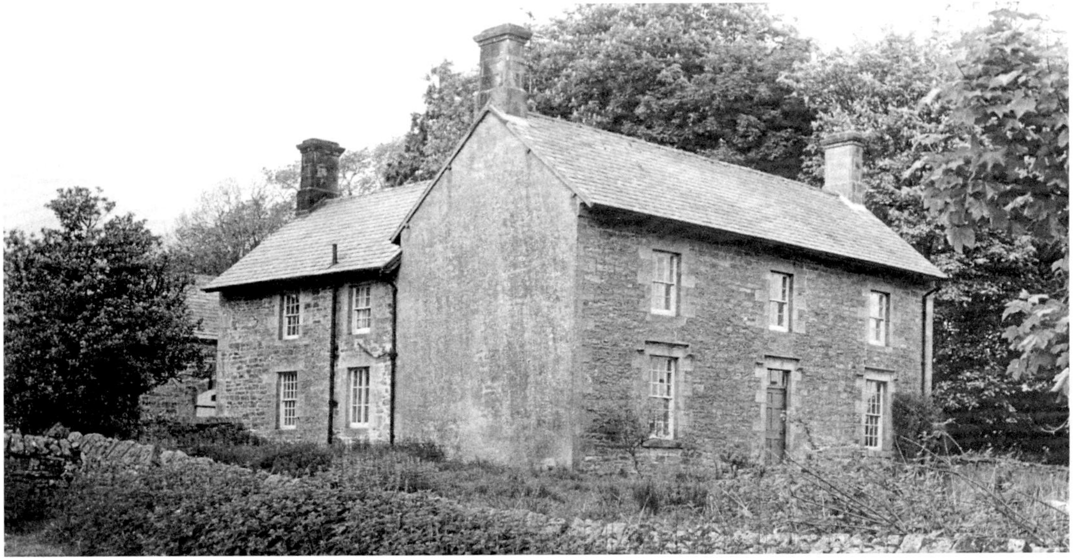

The Lost Houses of the North Tyne

Otterstone Lee was the pride of the farms owned by the Swinburne family of Capheaton Hall with its boundaries extending to the borders of Cumberland and Scotland. With its nine rooms and 9,000 acres of meadow and hill pasture, the farmhouse, three miles from Plashetts station, was at the centre of one of the largest sheep farms in England with its pastures divided into five hirsels of sheep: Leaplish, Lewisburn and Lishaw (High Long House), North Side and Yetburn (Low Long House).

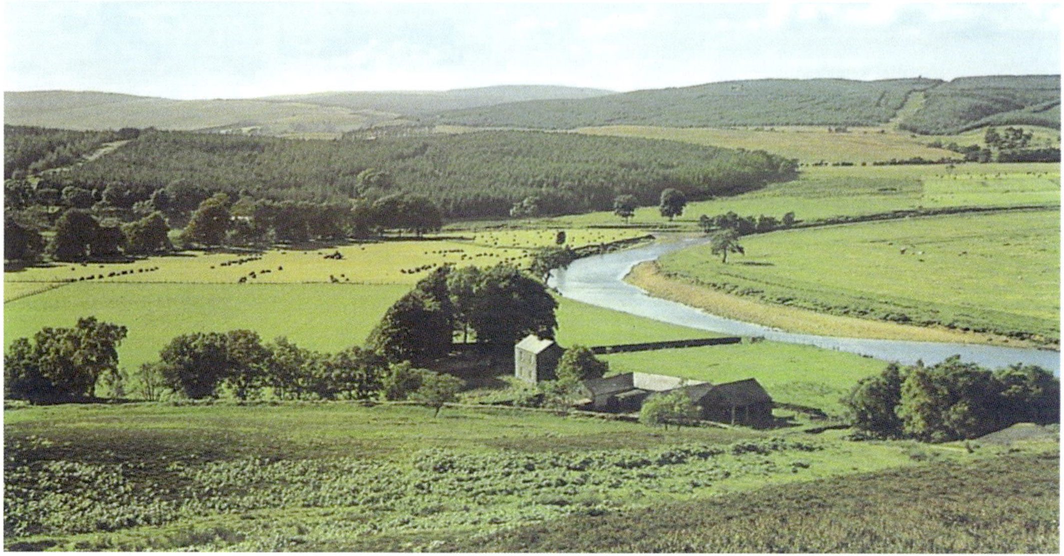

The Colour Postcards of the North Tyne

Shilburnhaugh Farm was one of nine working farms that were razed for the filling of Kielder Reservoir which began on 15th December 1980. In addition, over 30 Forestry Commission dwellings were demolished together with the hamlet at Plashetts station, the Lewisburn camp site and museum, smallholdings and cottages, amenity buildings, former hunting lodges, forestry workshops, Kielder Camp and tens of thousands of trees. The Reservoir was opened by Queen Elizabeth II on 26th May 1982.

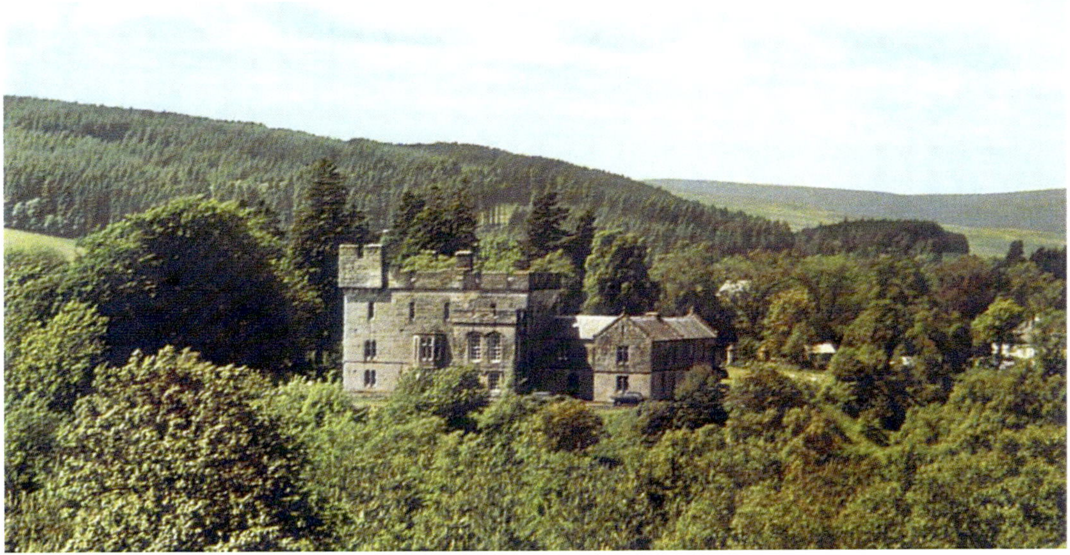

The Colour Postcards of the North Tyne

Kielder Castle was built between 1771 and 1775 as a hunting lodge for Hugh, 1st Duke of Northumberland. In Victorian times, his descendants would travel with members of their household in a special train from Alnwick Castle and used Kielder Castle to entertain shooting parties and the members of learned societies. The Kielder Estate was sold in 1932 to the Forestry Commission in lieu of heavy death duties. Valdemars Blankenburgs had his office within the castle as Surveyor and later as Clerk of Works.

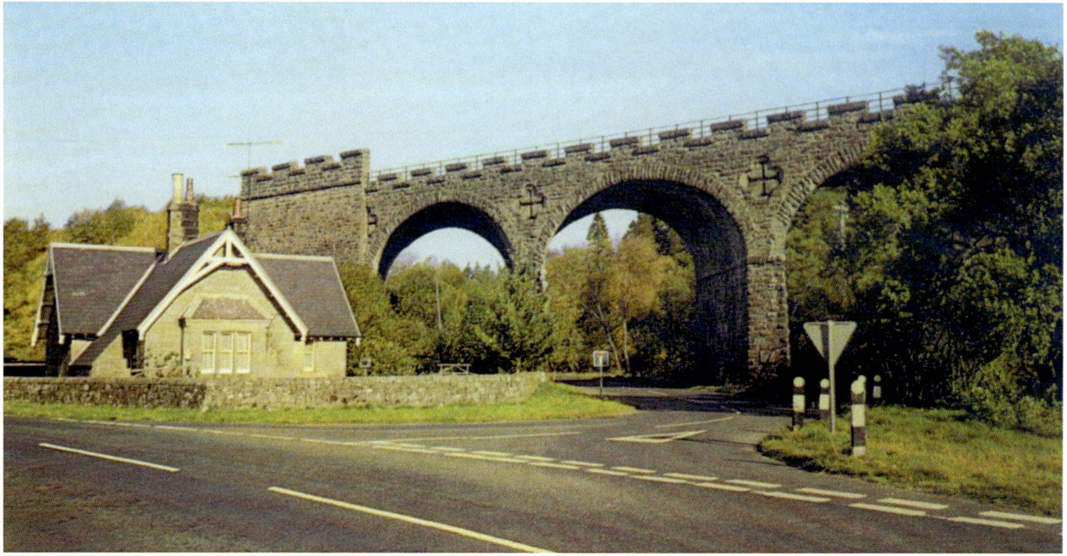

The Colour Postcards of the North Tyne

Kielder Viaduct was completed in 1864 to carry the Border Counties Railway from Hexham to Riccarton Junction where it connected with the Waverley Route from Edinburgh to Carlisle. Two special features of the viaduct are (1) the castellation demanded by the Duke of Northumberland so as to be in keeping with Kielder Castle and (2) the complicated skew-arch construction, which required the dimensions of each block of stone to be calculated mathematically and cut individually.

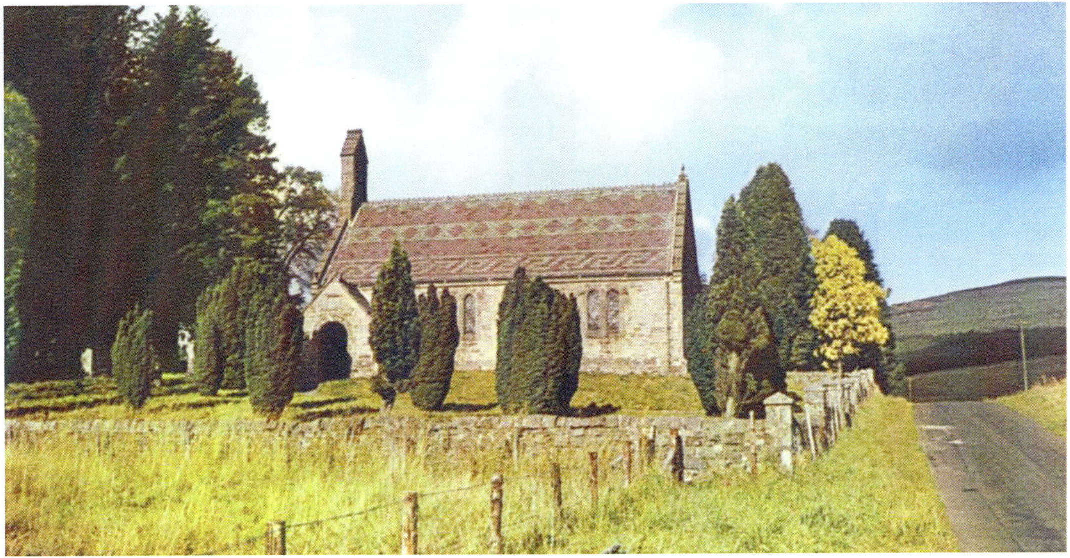

The Colour Postcards of the North Tyne

Kielder United Reformed Church is situated on the roadside just north of Kielder village and was given by the Duke of Northumberland in 1874 to replace a much earlier Presbyterian chapel at nearby Lightpipe Farm, dating back to 1709. The building is in the Early English style, built of sandstone with a slate roof, which has an interesting pattern of different coloured slates. The last burial took place in 2012 and the church closed for services in 2015. The church was sold for private development in 2017.

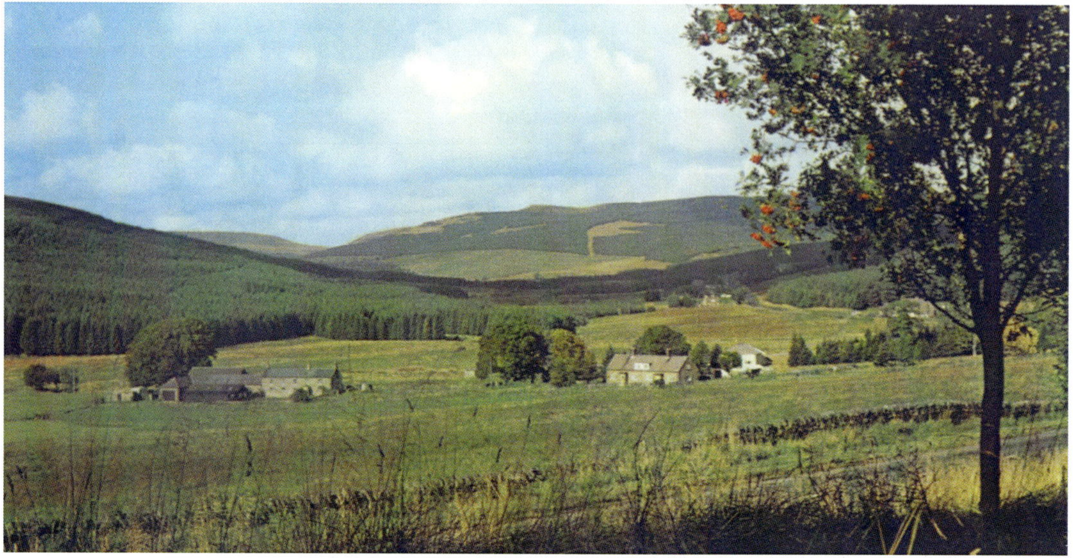

The Colour Postcards of Redesdale

This view of Redesdale on a fine day is exceptional and looks along Upper Redesdale towards Byrness Church and the Border at Carter Bar visible as a dip in the far distance. On the extreme left was Low Byrness, the home of Billy Bell (1862-1941), who was known as the Redesdale Bard. Hidden in the trees behind Cottonshopeburnfoot Farm was Byrness Summer Camp, another 1930s camp for the long-term unemployed. It was later used as a Prisoner of War Camp and then as a Forestry Commission depot.

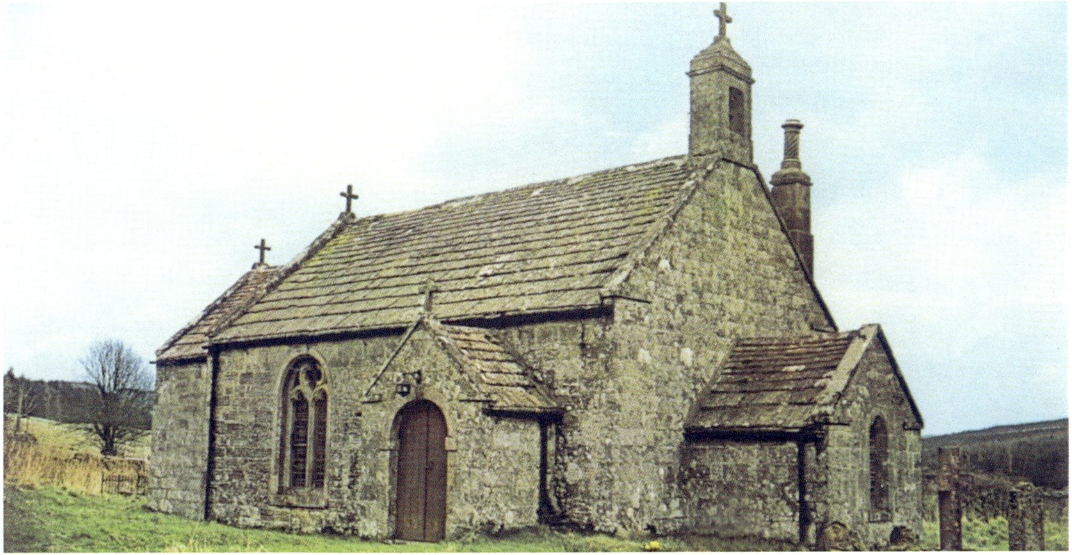

The Colour Postcards of Redesdale

The Church of St. Francis was built in 1793 and consecrated in 1796. It is unique because it shows a narrow-gauge industrial railway on a stained glass window, which was dedicated in 1903 in memory of the workmen who lived with their families at Catcleugh and built Catcleugh Reservoir between 1891 and 1905. In the churchyard is the touching iron memorial to George Carr who was killed aged 11 on 15th June 1901 while playing on the narrow-gauge railway that connected Catcleugh with Woodburn station.

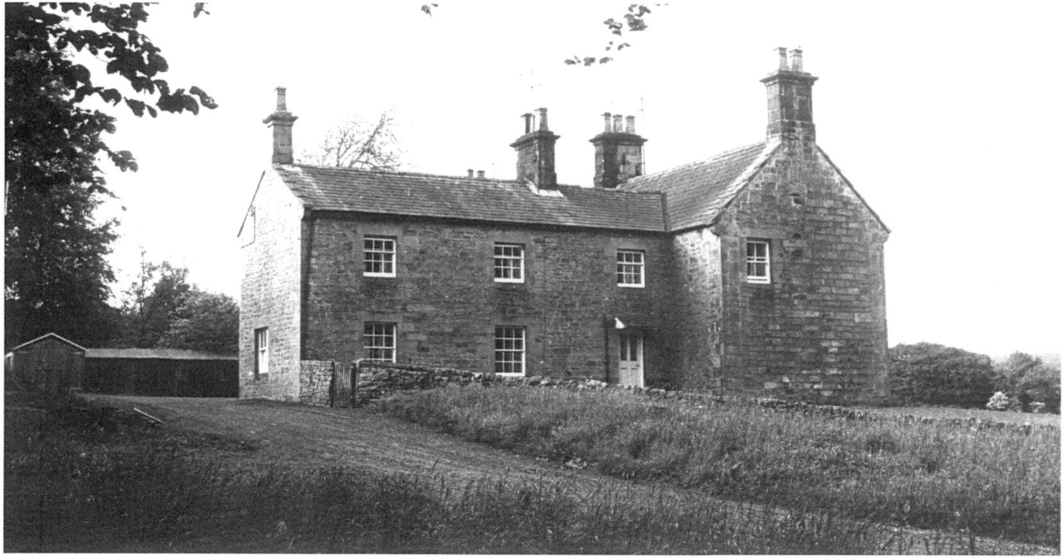

The Lost Houses of the North Tyne

Mounces Shooting Lodge: "With the shooting will be let this very comfortable and commodious mansion, comfortably furnished and comprising every necessary accommodation for a large party, with gardens, stables, and suitable appurtenances, beautifully situated in a bend of the North Tyne River, and adorned with the beautiful hanging woods of Leaplish. The house is situated about three miles from the Falstone Station and one mile from the Plashetts Station." [Bell's London Life 1866]

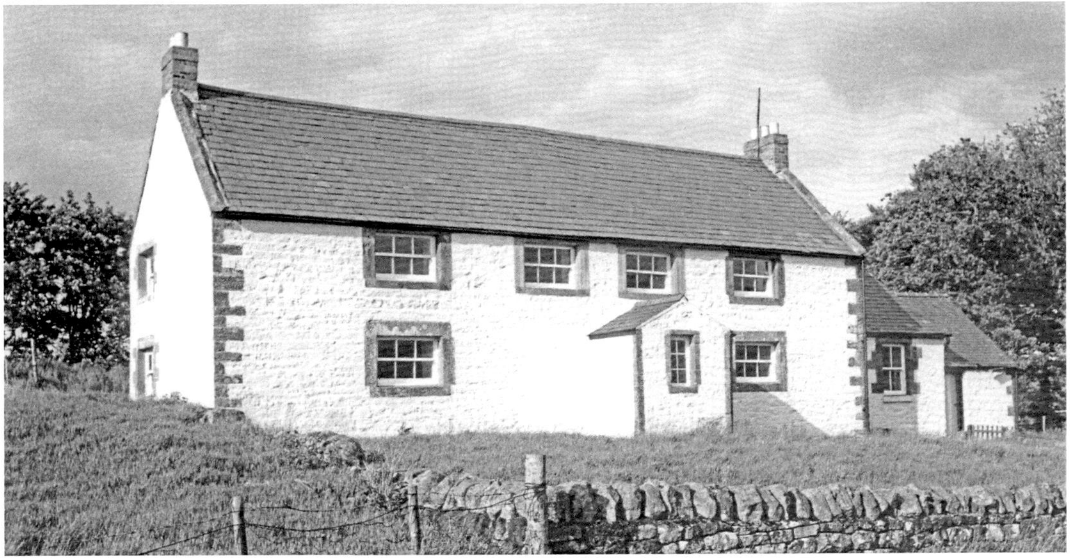

The Lost Houses of the North Tyne

Gamekeeper's Cottage: "The Mounces Estate commences about one mile from the Falstone Station on the Border Counties Railway and extends for upwards of 10 miles to the Scotch Border. The Estate is estimated to contain upwards of 25,000 acres and abounds with game. It is bounded for ten miles by the North Tyne River and intersected by various streams, abounding in fish. In the North Tyne, there is excellent salmon and other fishing: the other streams abound in trout." [Bell's London Life 1866]

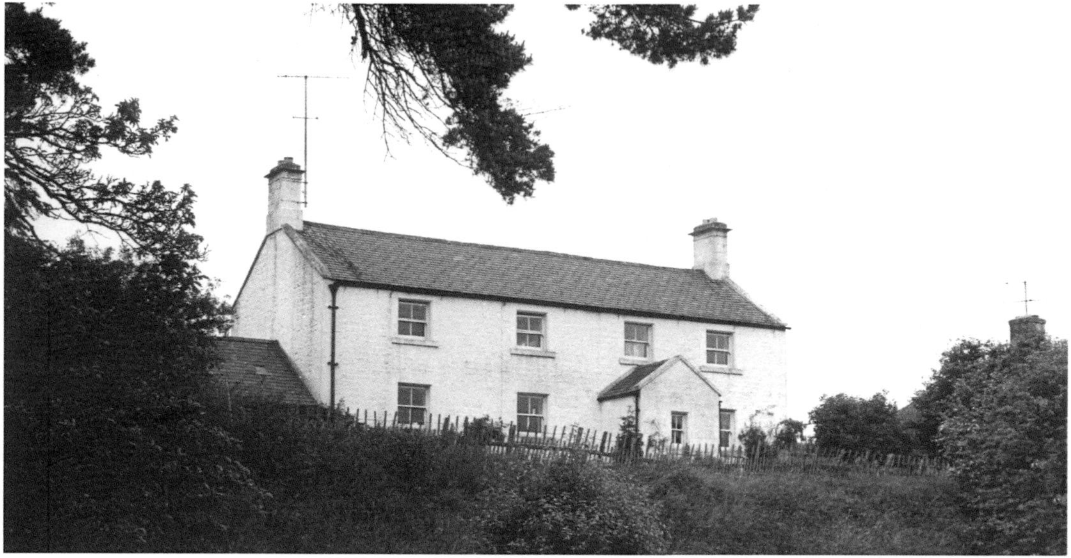

The Lost Houses of the North Tyne

Bakethin was the scene of a terrible accident on 27th July 1957 when John Terry, a 64-year-old forestry worker and smallholder of Bakethin, was killed by a train while walking along the track to tend his sheep and cows. Only two goods trains a day usually passed Bakethin but this engine was a special to Riccarton Junction to pick up a troop train. The train sounded its whistle but John Terry did not hear it because he was deaf. He had severe head injuries and a broken neck. His collie dog was cut in two.

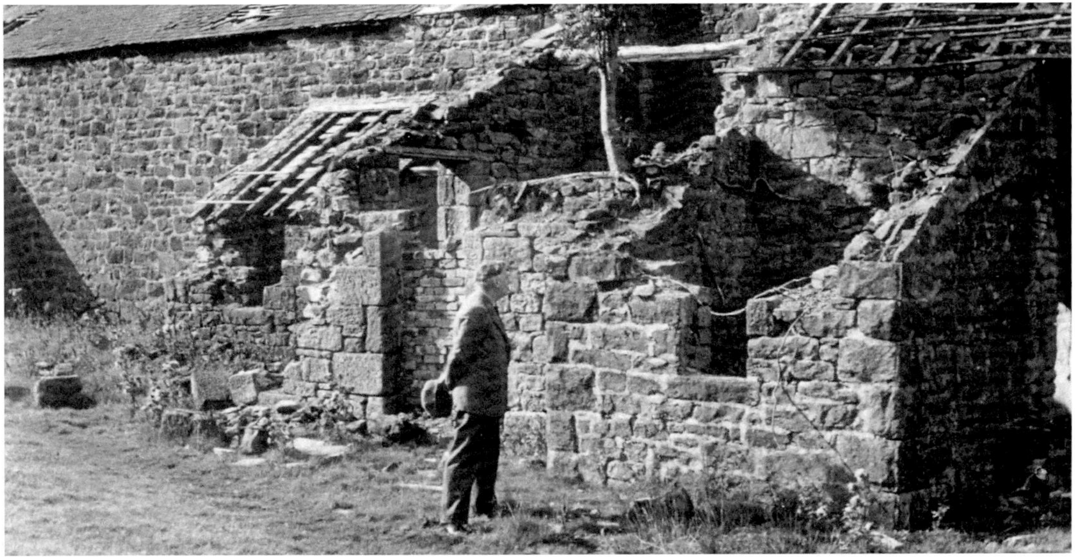

The Lost Houses of the North Tyne

Plashetts coal had been mined from early times but the opening of the railway in 1862 allowed mining on a commercial scale and the building of a colliery village in the hills. Mining flourished for many years but declined in the 1930s. Mining officially ceased in 1935 when Plashetts colliery village was abandoned. This photograph of one of the houses of Far Colliery was taken in the late 1950s just before the Forestry Commission demolished Far Colliery and all the other houses in the village in 1962.

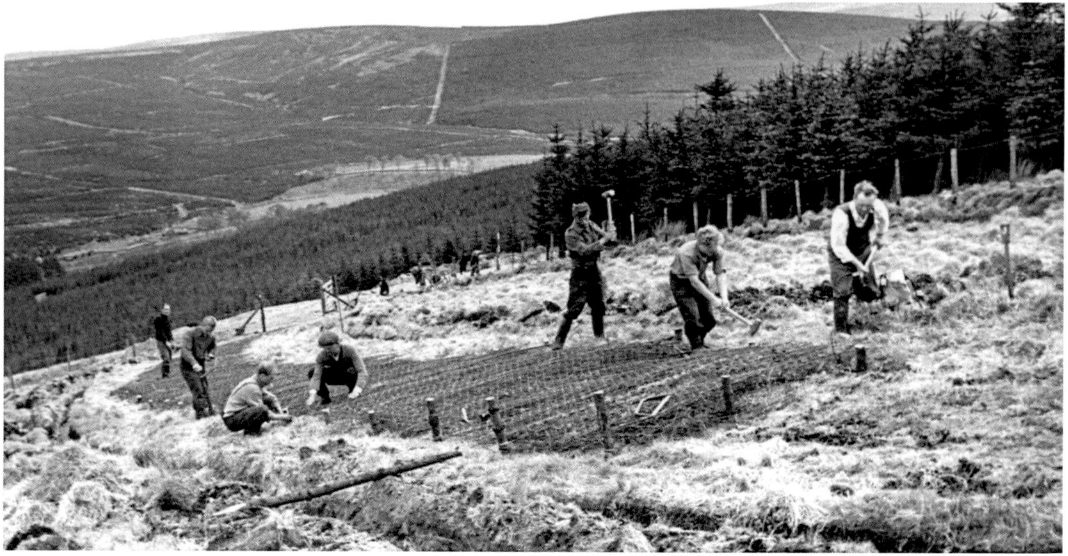

Latvians in the North Tyne

Latvians and Poles played a large part in the expansion of Kielder Forest for several years after World War Two and Valdemars Blankenburgs took many pictures of his fellow Latvians doing the jobs that he had prepared as a surveyor, opening up inaccessible and hitherto unplanted areas of Kielder. In this photograph of 1950, Latvians are building a temporary forestry road for fire fighting purposes. Even today, half of the land in Latvia is dedicated to forestry and timber production.

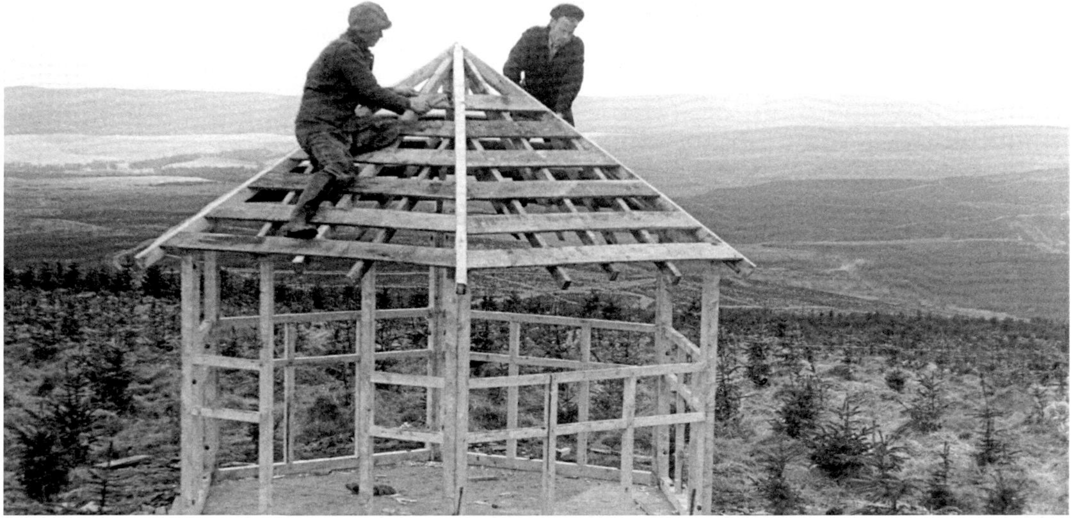

Latvians in the North Tyne

Latvians won a reputation for being hard-working and knowledgeable foresters who could turn their hands to road-making, fencing, planting and creating the infrastructure required by an expanding forest. Fire, however, remained an ever present threat to the forest and, until regular passenger trains ended on 13th October 1956, sparks from steam engines could easily cause lineside fires. In this photograph of 1950, two Latvian carpenters are building a fire-lookout cabin on the summit of a hill in Kielder Forest.

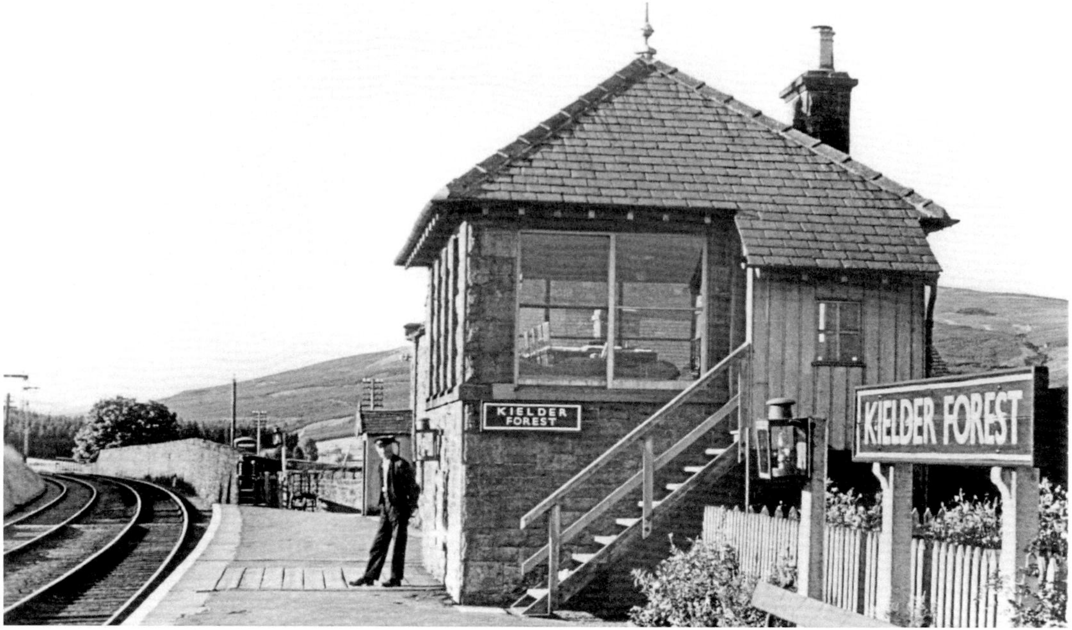

Kielder was renamed Kielder Forest on 1st October 1948 just three months after Lord Robinson had ceremoniously felled the first tree to be planted at Smale Farm in 1926. As he stood beside the new name boards, Valdemars Blankenburgs would have gained great pride and satisfaction from knowing that the area where he worked was now officially recognised as a Forest. This photograph was later produced as a postcard.

APPENDIX 1
LORD ROBINSON OF KIELDER FOREST AND OF ADELAIDE

On 15th July 1947, five months before the arrival of Valdemars Blankenburgs, Sir Roy Lister Robinson OBE was elevated to Lord Robinson, First Baron Robinson of Kielder Forest and of Adelaide, taking Adelaide as the place of his birth and Kielder because he was seen as the Father of the Forest and the guiding spirit of Border afforestation.

He began his forestry career in 1909 and was Chairman of the Forestry Commission from 1932 until his death in 1952. Having witnessed the planting of the first trees at Smale Farm in 1926, he returned in 1948 to fell the first tree that had grown large enough to be removed in the thinning of the oldest plantation. It was Valdemars Blankenburgs who preserved a record of the event. Just one photograph, perhaps, but his love of photography meant that from 1947 until his retirement in 1971, Valdemars Blankenburgs and his camera recorded virtually every stage in the development of Kielder Forest. One of the arguments for afforestation of the North Tyne Valley was that it changed the bare, bleak, windswept hills, where shepherds eked out a hard living, into a sustainable landscape, capable of supplying the universal demand for timber. A hundred trees, it was argued, could be planted on the two acres of land required to graze one sheep and the economic implications were obvious.

In December 1951, a few months before his death, Lord Robinson had written a short memoir of his recollections of Kielder which he first visited in 1921 on behalf of the newly formed Forestry Commission. There was a shortage of timber after the First World War and new areas were being urgently sought for afforestation. The North Tyne Valley seemed a suitable area and, after several sites had been explored and rejected, experimental planting began at Smale Farm in 1926. Results were initially disappointing but, with a subtle change in planting technique, results improved dramatically. Over the following years, Fortune smiled on Roy Robinson and his "creative energy and vision" for a forest in the Valley of the North Tyne.

From the earliest times, the most numerous occupants of the North Tyne Valley were shepherds. In 1951, this was still the case, as Lord Robinson noted in his memoir, when he observed that *"the old stone farm houses and occasional cottages stood as they had doubtless stood for very many years."* But, alongside the established occupation of the shepherd, the North Tyne Valley was subjected to waves of change, not least afforestation, which has made the Valley the most changed area in Northumberland.

On 27th May 1952, Valdemars Blankenburgs was at Butteryhaugh, recording Lord Robinson as he officially opened the new Forestry village, which added to the number of houses already occupied in the pre-war village of Castle Drive. A few months later, on 5th September 1952, Lord Robinson died of pneumonia while leading the British delegation to a Forestry Conference in Canada. His ashes were scattered at Whickhope Nick, deep in Kielder Forest, where a memorial cairn was unveiled on 29th September 1953, recording his great work for the Border woodlands, which are now his finest memorial. Valdemars Blankenburgs was present to record this event.

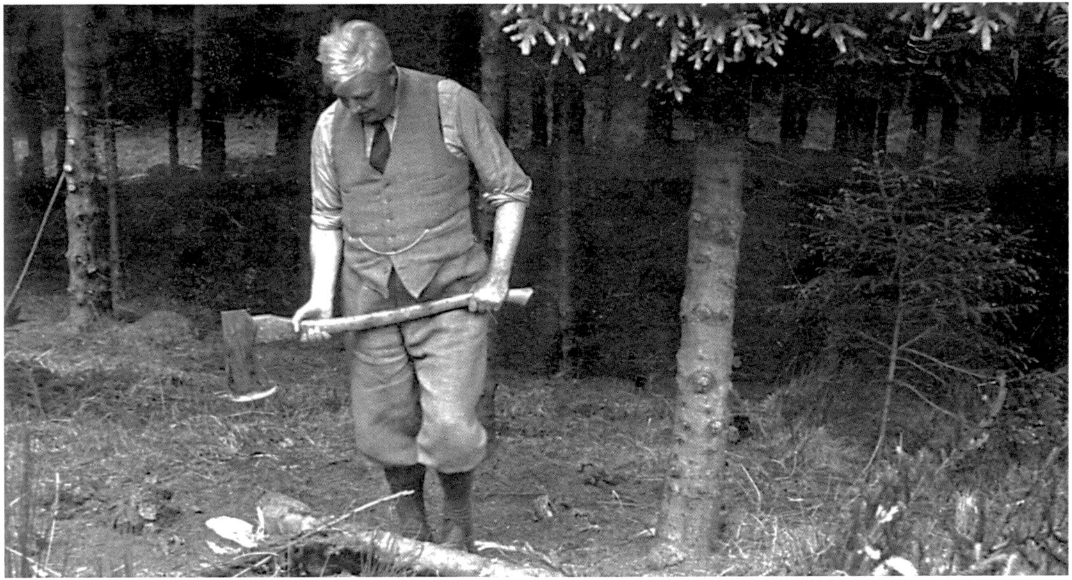

Roy Lister Robinson (1883-1952) This striking figure, seen on 2nd July 1948 felling the very first tree planted at Smale in 1926, came from his native Australia to Oxford University in 1905 as a Rhodes Scholar and gained academic and sporting distinction. From 1909, when he became an assistant inspector of forestry, he devoted his life to British forestry. He became the guiding spirit of the Forestry Commission upon its inception in 1919 and was its chairman from 1932 until his death in 1952.

APPENDIX 2
KIELDER 1939-1953

The outbreak of the Second World War saw more changes of population in and around Kielder. A wooden annex was added to Kielder School to accommodate Tyneside evacuees who lodged with local families but the biggest changes concerned Kielder Castle and Kielder Camp, the former Government Instructional Centre at Lewiefield.

KIELDER CASTLE 1939-1945

On 27th July 1940, the Newcastle Evening Chronicle reported that Kielder Castle was set to become a home for 60 aged and infirm ladies. Newcastle City Council would rent the Castle from the Forestry Commission, its new owners, for the duration of the war. It was stated that 40 old and infirm cases were in Hexham Poor Law Institution and 20 at Elswick Grange Workhouse. The Hexham institution was now required for emergency hospital purposes and the committee had been requested to move the Newcastle cases without delay. With regard to Elswick Grange, the committee had handed over to the Health Committee at the outbreak of war 433 beds for emergency purposes with the result that the accommodation for institutional cases had become taxed to the limit.

It seems that many of the new residents were overwhelmed by the size and grandeur of their new accommodation. Every one of their rooms was a “room with a view” commanding huge sweeps of rugged, heather-clad hill and fell. The only problem was a continuing need for staff as many recruits found that they could not cope with the isolation of Kielder and advertisements regularly appeared in the local newspapers.

The old ladies of the Tyne found Kielder Castle a safe haven and, on 9th November 1940, the Newcastle Weekly Chronicle carried a picture of three elderly residents with two nurses sitting in a quiet corner of the castle grounds where they were happily knitting. On 3rd March 1944, a reporter from the Daily Mirror visited Kielder and published a touching article:

"These grey-haired women with buckled hands and rounded shoulders have left their industrial heritage, which was the workhouse in Newcastle, and have settled down comfortably in one of the Duke of Northumberland's former castles at Kielder. They are the mothers and grandmothers of the fitters and shipbuilders of the Tyne and most of them told me that they would like to be back looking at the Tyne. Kielder Castle was used by the Duke during the shooting season but now it is used all the year round by 65 old ladies transferred from the Elswick Grange Workhouse.

The ladies are so old, most being seventy and eighty years of age, that they are not unduly impressed by the home they have found. Even the boudoir of the duchess that once held one dainty chintz-covered bed now has six black iron bedsteads in it. I saw these old women in their castle having tea on trestle tables in the long hall that had been used for the Duke of Northumberland's dinner parties. They were eating bread and jam. When they had eaten, they did not move and, at each of the long tables, they began to pour the tea dregs into their saucers. They began to tell fortunes from the tea leaves as they do every afternoon, as they have done all their years."

KIELDER CAMP 1939-1953

During the Second World War and in the immediate post-war years, the former Government Instructional Centre became home to three successive groups of people: Newfoundland lumberjacks, ratings of the Royal Navy with mental health issues and, finally, European Voluntary Workers and Displaced Persons from war-torn Europe.

1 NEWFOUNDLAND LUMBERJACKS 1939-1941

At the outbreak of the Second World War, the Government Instructional Centre closed and the site became home to 200 Newfoundland lumberjacks, who made a great impression when "clad in the picturesque garb of the Canadian lumberjack" they spent a Saturday in Hawick on 17th February 1940. They claimed that working conditions at Kielder were better than those in Newfoundland.

Timber was a key home-grown raw material in wartime Britain. However, extracting it from inhospitable areas was quite a significant headache for the authorities since conscription had removed many professional foresters and, as a result, there was an immediate scarcity of home-grown labour. Many of these timber-rich areas were in Scotland, not least in East Lothian, and two significant groups of foreign workers were recruited to plug the gap and to bolster the extraction effort: the first came from Newfoundland and the second from British Honduras, now Belize, which was the only British colony in Central America.

Overseas supplies of raw timber became severely restricted during the Second World War, as the German navy attempted to isolate the British Isles by disrupting the convoys bringing essential supplies by sea, forcing the country to satisfy demands for material such as timber from local resources. However, this problem was not restricted only to material resources. Labour was also in short supply, as many men had been conscripted into the Armed Forces. This shortfall in labour was addressed by calling on overseas assistance and by the creation in April 1942 of the Women's Timber Corps, whose recruits, known as Lumberjills, worked in woodlands and forests like Kielder.

The Newfoundland Overseas Forestry Unit was active between 1939 and 1946. The unit was created on 17th November 1939, when a radio announcement was made by the Canadian Commissioner for Natural Resources, appealing for volunteer loggers to work in Great Britain.

The scarcity of trained forestry workers in the UK had led to a call for volunteers from Newfoundland, Great Britain's first unofficial colony overseas. Strong traditional ties bound Newfoundland with the 'Mother Country' and the call was quickly answered, with a force of some 300 men arriving in Liverpool on the 18th December 1939 and a full contingent of 2,150 arriving by February 1940. Records indicate that a total of approximately 3,680 men were recruited. Thirty-four died as a result of accidents or illness and 540 of them later enlisted in the British Armed Forces.

The men were paid $2.00 per day, or $12.00 week, from which a compulsory deduction of $1.00 per day was made and forwarded to their families in Newfoundland. Although the men who answered the call were provided with transport, accommodation and medical services as part of the deal, personal needs, such as clothing, were their own responsibility, for which they had to make their own arrangements.

The final group of foresters returned to Newfoundland on 26th July 1946, having been asked by the British Government to remain at their work for a further year after the end of the war. Early in the war a group of these men came to Elmscleugh, near Dunbar, where they worked in local forests for some five months before moving north to areas around Inverness. The timber extracted was used largely for pit props, pier repairs and for beach defences.

One of the Newfoundland volunteers was Lewis Jenkins, aged twenty, who arrived with the first group in 1939. He went home after the war but, finding no suitable work, returned and remained to live in the Dunbar area. Lewis was unusual in one respect: a tussle at school over a pencil had gone very wrong and the pencil had pierced his left eye. He had lost the eye but this did not stop him from turning into a good forester and from becoming an accurate shot with a rifle. Lewis gave this account of his experiences:

"We were born in Britain's oldest colony and when they called for volunteers for the forestry, well, that's why we volunteered. Three hundred of us came over in the first group, landed at Liverpool and went by train to Kielder. We were at Kielder Camp for eight or nine months, cutting timber at Mounces and Plashetts to keep the mines going. The miners needed pit props and other timber to keep the roof up in those days. I began as a cook and then became a lumberjack.

After we had finished at Kielder, we went to Castle O'er, near Eskdalemuir. We cut out some wood there and then we landed up in Elmscleugh, near Dunbar. There was a lot of timber there. We sent wood all over England and we cut the timber for the sands at Belhaven. This was all done to stop the Germans landing or dropping in men. In Elmscleugh, we cut the timber and loaded it on to trailers and wagons and it went down to England.

Our food was rationed like everything else in the UK. We had one egg a week and two ounces of butter a month. Lunch was three slices of bread and a tin of corned beef. We had to sweeten our tea with strawberry jam. The huts we lived in were wooden and in the winter the inside walls were white with frost. We used paraffin lamps at night and provided our own entertainment.

We were about five to six months in Elmscleugh and then we had to shift up north to just north of Inverness. We had our own sawmills up there. We never returned to Elmscleugh and, when it was all over, we were told overnight that we were going to

Liverpool and then back home. When I got home, I found that the only work was in the timber trade and so I returned to Scotland. I worked in the timber business with Dickson and after that I worked at the Belhaven Brewery for twenty-eight years."

2 DISTRESSED NAVAL PERSONNEL 1942-1945

Between 1942 and 1945, Kielder Camp became HMS Standard, a shore establishment of the Royal Navy, equipped to assess and rehabilitate naval personnel with personality disorders, locally known as the Royal Naval Labour Camp for neurotic ratings.

By 1941, the Royal Navy had been growing increasingly concerned about the number of men suffering from behavioural problems, which prevented them from carrying out full duties. Several locations were considered before it was decided to take over the now deserted labour camp near Kielder. Although the camp was taken over in 1941, it was not until early 1942 that the first men were posted there. A substantial Guard House was built at the entrance to the camp and a large car park was created in front of the Flagpole to make a quarterdeck. A Nissan Hut on the extreme perimeter of the camp was converted into the padded cell unit where those considered to be in danger of injuring themselves to get discharge would be kept in straightjackets for a few days.

The base was not a hospital. It was under the command of officers of the Royal Navy Executive Branch rather than the Royal Navy Medical Service, although two Royal Navy psychiatrists were assigned to the staff. The men fell into three categories: those with low morale, those of temperamental instability, and malingerers. The aim was to return these men not necessarily to active service but to some form of effective war service. The regime of the base put an emphasis on physical labour and education to support the overall aim of returning the men to effective service. Rather than a general regime, each man was assessed and a personalised regime of work, recreation and education was established.

During the three years that HMS Standard was operational, 842 men were assessed of whom 680 were classed as 'successes' because they were drafted to other duties within the Navy with the average stay at HMS Standard being four months. Of those redrafted, the records are incomplete but some performed well enough to be decorated, while over 100 were the subject later in their service careers of bad reports. The remaining 162 men were all discharged from the Navy.

Ronald Milton worked in the Stores at HMS Standard between January and October 1942 and describes the photograph that W. P. Collier took in the late 1930s when it was still a Government Instructional Centre for the long-term unemployed.

"As you can see from the photograph, it was a large camp of substantial buildings. Two women lived in the stone building on the right alongside the main road. Opposite, at the entrance into the camp, was built a very substantial Guard House. The end of the second Hut was our office and sleeping accommodation was the last Hut at the front of the photograph. A large car park in front of the Flagpole was created to make a quarterdeck.

The padded cell unit was created in a Nissan Hut to the extreme left just off the photograph. Those considered to be suspect of injuring themselves in order to get discharged were kept in straightjackets in a padded cell for a few days."

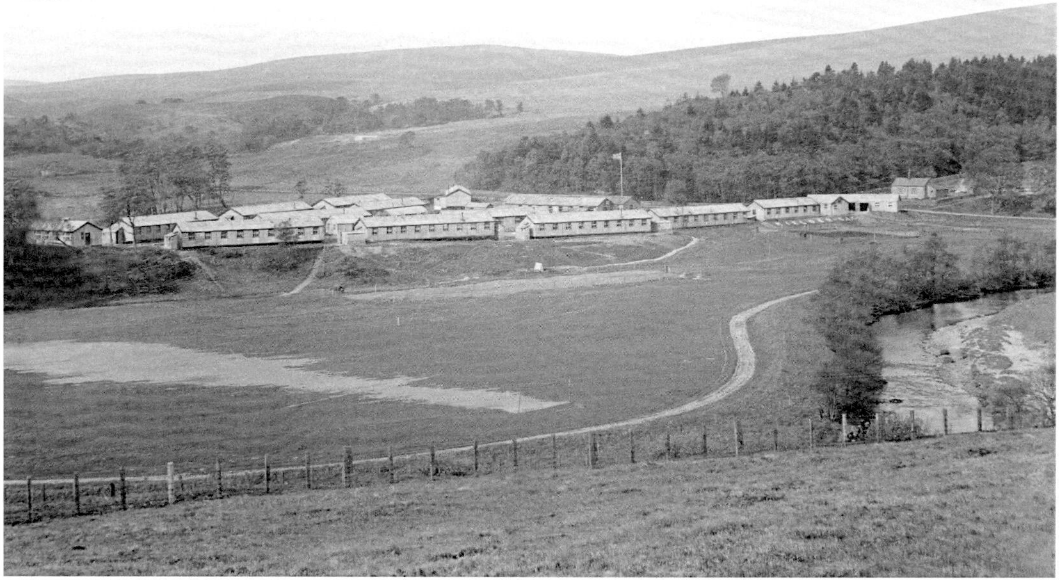

3 EUROPEAN VOLUNTARY WORKERS & DISPLACED PERSONS 1947-1953

The months following the end of hostilities in 1945 soon revealed that there were not enough British workers to fill the millions of job vacancies required to rebuild war-torn Britain. In 1947, therefore, the British Ministry of Labour and National Service started recruiting drives in the DP (Displaced Persons) camps in Germany where there were over 10 million refugees, who had fled from countries seized by the Russians.

Single able-bodied workers were the preferred recruits with Latvian women being particularly desirable because they were *"scrupulously clean in their persons and habits, and full of the spirit and stuff of which we can make Britons."* Married men had to leave their wives behind in Germany, having been promised that permission would be granted for wives to join their husbands very soon thereafter. Conditions in the DP camps were deteriorating: the Germans resented the DPs and there was no prospect of finding a decent future in Germany. The result was that some 25,000 refugees from the Baltics signed up as EVWs (European Voluntary Workers). EVWs were paid the same wages as British workers in similar jobs but faced some hostility and discrimination, being barred from applying for skilled jobs by some trade unions. They were housed in "work hostels" which were often ex-army Nissen huts, some of which had held prisoners-of-war.

Kielder Forest, needing many more manual workers as well as specialists, had recruited some of the remnants of the Polish Army of Wladyslaw Anders, a general in the Polish Army and later in life a politician and member of the Polish government-in-exile in

London. They were given preferential treatment before other Displaced Persons for jobs in forestry since they had fought so valiantly with the British army. General Anders later wrote about his army's amazing odyssey from battles against the Germans in Poland, prison camps in Russia to exile in England via Iran, Iraq, and Palestine where they passed under British command to fight in Italy, capturing Monte Cassino, and the final spring offensive in Northern Italy.

At Kielder, the Polish ex-soldiers were housed in the huts recently vacated by the personnel of HMS Standard. Other Eastern Europeans, mainly from Latvia, which has always been rich in forests, arrived later to boost the workforce. The harsh conditions, low wages and lack of social life and entertainment eventually led to an exodus of many of the EVWs, who found better prospects in the towns and cities.

By 1952, the Forestry Commission had decided, on the grounds of economy, to close Kielder Camp, known as "The Foreign Village in the Forest" where about 100 forestry workers of various nationalities had been living. The British workers at the camp would continue to be employed by the Forestry Commission but would have to find alternative accommodation while around 80 European Voluntary Workers would become redundant. Most of the European Voluntary Workers were sorry to leave: one of the men from Yugoslavia had been at the camp for 16 months.

A Forestry Commission official said that the closing of the camp would not affect the work in Kielder Forest, with planting, thinning and fire protection measures continuing as usual. Most of the regular workers were already living in Forestry Commission houses, farm houses and shepherds' cottages in the district. New Forestry Commission houses at Butteryhaugh were being completed and occupied.

On 24th January 1953, the end came to Kielder Camp, a unique and truly diverse community in the middle of Kielder Forest, where Poles, Latvians and other European Voluntary Workers, employed by the Forestry Commission, had lived for some time. Only the cook and maintenance men were staying on but they too would be going in a couple of weeks when the camp was finally closed.

The dismissed workers found jobs all over England and the little community established at Kielder was now completely broken. Fourteen were to work at a bacon factory in Wiltshire, others at quarries at Barrasford, near Hexham, and some found jobs with a steel firm at Scunthorpe. A few were going to work for a Polish-run firm of forestry contractors who operated in Northumberland.

In a statement made to the Newcastle Journal of 19th January 1953, Mr. R. E. Crowther, appointed in 1950 as District Officer for Kielder Forest, confirmed that orders for a cut in the expenditure of the Forestry Commission had been given. "Someone had to go and it was decided that the European Voluntary Workers should be the first. The Poles at Kielder Camp include men who served in the Polish Army and have been at Kielder since 1947. They are naturally sorry to leave but we cannot do anything about it. The huts are old and, in my opinion, it will be no great loss if they are pulled down."

In fact, Kielder Camp was not pulled down. For the next 25 years, it was used as a Forestry Commission workshop until it was submerged beneath the waters of Kielder Reservoir. The Forestry Commission made similar use of the former Government Instructional Summer Camp at Byrness and closed it at about the same time.

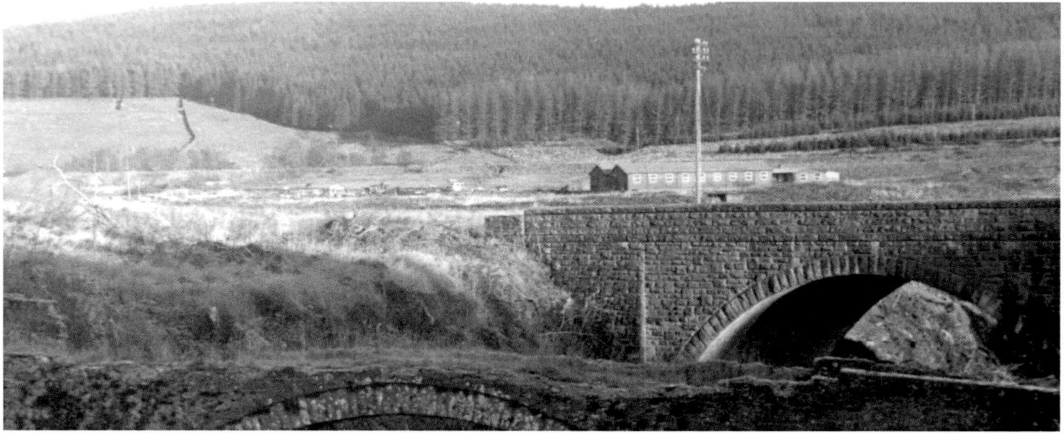

This photograph, taken by retired forester Arthur Taylor in 1980, shows the old bridge at Lewisburn in the foreground and the new bridge that replaced it during the 1930s. In the background are two of the former camp huts which the Auxiliary Fire Service joined together and heightened to store their vehicles. Behind them is the hut of the Commandant, with the hill leading up to Gowanburn Farm on the top left.

APPENDIX 3
KIELDER FOREST IN 1947
A YEAR TO REMEMBER

With snow lasting from January until April, the year 1947 had endured one of the most severe winters on record when Valdemars Blankenburgs arrived at Kielder on 8th December to begin his job as a surveyor. It was the year when the Forestry Commission would launch an extensive post-war programme of expansion and planting.

Several factors in post-war Britain ensured that the arrival of Valdemars Blankenburgs at Kielder was both opportune and welcome as thoughts turned to securing future timber production just as it had after the First World War. Vast amounts of timber had been used for military purposes during the War and what remained was now being used to repair bomb-damaged houses and factories. Even the trees along the Hareshaw Burn at Bellingham had been harvested for the war effort. Planting at Kielder had been hindered, not halted, by the Second World War, as shown by the forestry housing development at Castle Drive, but future development of Kielder Forest would require careful planning.

Valdemars Blankenburgs fitted the job admirably despite, as he admitted, his limited knowledge of English. It was knowledge of land, however, rather than language that was more important. Monday 8th December 1947 was when he began work at Kielder and where he would work until his retirement as Clerk of Works on 26th February 1971.

16th June: The Empire Forestry Conference opened in London and about 100 delegates and associate delegates were to visit a number of State and private forests in order to see something of the work that was being done to extend Britain's woodlands. It was anticipated that, by the time that the delegates visited the forests of the Borders, the 49,000,000th tree would have been planted at Kielder and Redesdale, which was more than one tree per head of the population of Great Britain.

15th July: Sir Roy Lister Robinson OBE was elevated to Lord Robinson, First Baron Robinson of Kielder Forest and of Adelaide, taking Adelaide as the place of his birth and Kielder because he was seen as the Father of the Forest. In 1932, he had been made Chairman of the Forestry Commission, a post that he held until his death in 1952.

One of his arguments for the afforestation of the North Tyne Valley was that it could change the bare, bleak, windswept hills, where shepherds eked out a hard living, into a sustainable landscape, capable of supplying the universal demand for timber. A hundred trees, it was argued, could be planted on the two acres of land required to graze one sheep and the economic implications were obvious.

14th November: Three weeks before Valdemars Blankenburgs arrived at Kielder, the Daily Mirror published a long article entitled *"Getting out of the Wood"* in which it celebrated the importance of forests to rebuild Britain and to make up for the heavy felling of woodlands during two World Wars. These forests would occupy large tracts of land in Northumberland, Cumberland, Dumfriesshire and Roxburghshire.

"Across the Border between England and Scotland," the Mirror revealed, "foresters were doing the biggest job of landscape gardening in British history. *'There's gold in Britain's once barren northern hills – gold that grows from the ground in the shape of trees.'* They were planning for the future: spruce and pine trees were growing on land that had been moorland and bog for three or four centuries.

The largest one-unit place was in Northumberland, where the Kielder, Redesdale and Wark Forests ran one into the other and would march for five miles along the Roman Wall with the projected National Park. Stanley Rogers was the Forestry Commission's District Officer for these three forests. He had 31,000 acres already growing trees and 40,000 acres were still to be planted. Sitka and Norway spruce and Scots pine, which grew to maturity in 80 years, made up the bulk of the planting.

This young Londoner, still in his thirties, planned for thirty years ahead when the forest would be in full timber production. At the present time, he had fewer than 200 workers in his district. In 1957, he would have nearly 500; in 1967, more than 1,000; and by 1977 close on 3,000 living in eight villages specially built to house the foresters and woodsmen, engineers and mechanics and their families. By the time the forest was complete, Rogers estimated that between 250 and 500 miles of roads would be needed in his area alone to get the timber harvest away each year. In two years' time, axes would begin to ring in earnest when he started timber production: pit props from the thinnings of the first 45 acres planted at Smale Farm where the idea of a Border Forest at Kielder was first conceived in 1926.

The final answer lay in the value of those hills to the nation. Well stocked by sheep, they could produce twice their previous value as sheep runs. The Forestry Commission acquired their land in the years between the wars when hill farming was a thankless and profitless task. Under timber, they would produce ten times the sheep value every year, for when a forest was in full growth, it produced not only timber for sawmills and pulp but the thinnings of the growing plantations gave pit props, scaffolding poles, telegraph poles and small timber for a hundred and one uses.

When the Border Forests were completed in ten or twenty years' time, there would be sixteen of them, stretching 60 miles east and west from Otterburn to Dumfries and 32 miles north and south between Hawick and the Roman Wall.

This would be the largest forest area in the British Isles, with 107,000 acres of plantable land. It made the British taxpayer, through the Forestry Commission, the biggest landowner in these parts, holding 160,000 acres of farm, moor and forest.

Stanley Rogers intended to plant 3,900 acres of Kielder, Redesdale and Wark. To do this, he needed 7,000,000 plants. They would come from seed harvested in Canada in 1941, brought to Britain in 1942 and sown in forest nurseries in 1943. The job would cost about £8 an acre.

Today, huge crawler tractors pull ploughs turning over great strips of turf at whatever distance apart the trees are to be planted, usually five feet. This does a double job:

the deep, wide furrow acts as a drainage trench. Then along come the forest workers with special narrow spades; they cut holes in the turf, plant the trees and firm them with their feet, as rapidly as the market gardener plants his cabbages.

Sheep farmers complain that the forest men grab the best land and leave bare the tops of the fells. Stanley Rogers is doing his best to disprove this in his three forests: pines and spruces, planted last year in a 20-acre peat bog, are all doing well.

Rogers is planting up to 1,300 feet above sea level and reckons that he will be able to plant all but 200 acres of the tops of the hills in his district. At one point, on Carter Fell, the Forestry Commission is leaving a 500-acre farm for breeding hill sheep. Elsewhere, the best land near the old Cheviot farmsteads is kept for food production.

A properly managed forest could go on producing timber like this forever, though foresters could rarely live long enough to see the completion of their work. This was part of the fascination of the forest."

The paper left its readers with the final thoughts of Stanley Rogers: "We are working for the future. Except for fire, things do not happen quickly in the forest and so we always have time to think out the next move."

[The figures quoted by Stanley Rogers in 1947 for foresters and forestry villages never materialised as mechanisation quickly reduced the numbers of workers required]

APPENDIX 4

Two letters from Valdemars in Britain to his wife Elfrida in Germany
Translated from Latvian by Maija Robinson (née Blankenburgs)

30th May 1947 Full Sutton, near Stamford Bridge

My dear,
So far away and I'm sunning myself in central England and can describe to you my first impressions I have gained about this country's people, landscape and general conditions. But first, a few words about the journey in chronological order.

We reached Hull after a journey of 2 or 3 hours on a very calm sea. Nobody, not even the women, was sick. We got there about 9.00 p.m. We didn't disembark and it was only after breakfast next morning that our journey started. During the crossing we heard a lot about how English Customs would look at our hand luggage. That indeed happened and we were led through Customs carrying our hand luggage and nowhere were we stopped. By contrast, the English soldiers who were the majority of the passengers on our ship, were checked very thoroughly and we saw the things the Customs men had taken out which had to have duty paid on them – cameras, hunting rifles. Next came the Customs inspection of the baggage. On the harbour were great heaps of boxes with our belongings, which in size were equal to 3 or 4 of our wood piles heaped together. Four Customs men approached with great dignity, with a workman, who carried a lot of specialist tools for opening boxes. A medium sized box was opened and, after a cursory look inside at its contents, it was carefully nailed up again, and in the same dignified way in which they had arrived, the English Customs men departed. That was the end of the baggage control.

Having loaded the baggage ourselves onto trucks, we climbed into a double-decker bus and set off for the transit camp on the outskirts of Hull. There we were put into comfortable barracks for 12 people. Everyone had a bed and 3 blankets. Then we had lunch and were given a first present from the English nation – everyone was given 15/- pocket money (purchasing power of 15 Lats back in independent Latvia!) a knife, fork, spoons and a towel.

In this camp, I also met 2 friends from Greven[1], who are still waiting to be assigned to a job. In the evening, according to camp tradition, the different national groups put on a performance. The Latvians quickly formed a choir and sang a couple of songs. I think our rendition of "Put Vējiņ" (Blow Gentle Wind) was the high point of the evening. The camp director, a very nice retired captain (English!) declared in his speech that, as we were on free British soil, we could freely sing our songs and be political about our occupation. "I would like you to close this evening's concert with your country's national anthem" he said at the end of his speech. Of course, this was done with great enthusiasm.

The next morning, we travelled by bus to the work dispersement camp. Here we will have to stay until we get work. This apparently will take 2 to 3 weeks. Here we found many of our friends from Greven, who still have not been assigned to a job. It seems that the English also approach this task very unhurriedly. First, the Labour Commission appears, who ask yet again what job each person is able to do, and what they would like to do. Greven's i.e. German Commissioners' reports are not looked at all. They say that the Commission will arrive next week at our camp. Then their reports go to London and then from there will come the directives. Up to now, the only ones who have got jobs, with a few exceptions, are in agriculture and animal husbandry. The women go to hospitals and textile factories.

And now a few words about England generally, however correct my first impressions may be. Because of the large number of inhabitants per square km, I thought England would be densely built-up, crowded with factories, houses, smoking chimneys and, above all, constant fog "without sun or stars". Perhaps that's how it is in London, and perhaps here in the past, but what I saw from the bus journey from Hull to Full Sutton, to me (and all the others!) it came as a complete and pleasant surprise. Nature and, I think, people's actions relating to it, here in the countryside around York is more similar to Latvia than that in Westphalia (i.e. around Greven).

First of all, many old large trees, not only around houses (detached!) but also along the sides of ditches, in fields, pastures, clearings. Along the roadsides the English don't like fences but we often see hedges which are artificially made into bushes in a naturalistic manner and pleasing to the eye. Above all, we see a lot of pastures (tidy!) and fields which are pleasant to look at with their greenery. Along the road sides, there are grass verges 3 to 5 metres wide, unlike in Germany where the tarmac ends at a ditch. The roads are all tarmacked, even the minor ones, but they also distinguish themselves pleasantly from Germany's roads in that they are not dead straight, as though a rope had been stretched, but with nice bends which together with the green verges and hedges fit very nicely in the landscape.

All in all, the English landscape is more natural, beautiful and less ruthlessly exploited than we see in Germany, especially Westphalia. This particularly pleases me because a lot of places are like a beautiful park! Also in England there is not the dearth of birds that there is in Germany. In every bush we hear birds chirping, cuckoos echo all around and in the field, where I am sitting and writing at this moment, I can hear uninterrupted birdsong. Regarding the climate, at the moment it is very pleasant. For many weeks, it has been summer without interruption and at the moment it is quite hot. That is not unusual; so as to fog and rain, at least in middle England, that has been exaggerated.

Our camp is about 70 km west of Hull, completely in the countryside, some 4km from a small town and 15km from the main city of York. To the east, about 5km away, there is a hilly area which protects us from the North Sea winds. The camp (which is called a "hostel" not camp as in Germany) is in the former army camp which consists of rounded metal barracks (Nissen Huts) very tidy and comfortable with all conveniences. Nice washrooms with hot showers. There are about 400 such buildings, also massive central admin buildings, kitchens, libraries, meeting rooms, etc. The barracks aren't close together but in small groups, separated by lawns and hedges so they are completely separated from each other. The barrack size is 5m x 11m, usually housing 10 people, so each person has about 5.5 sq. m. The barracks in each group of about 20 to 30 are rather more close together but there are asphalt paths between, with plenty of grass.

In our barrack are four of our Latvian friends from Greven. The rest are also Latvians and decent people. It's noteworthy that, in all this time, nobody has lost anything, nothing has been stolen, even though our things, e.g. in Hull, stood for hours unlocked in the barracks when there was a lot of coming and going for hours without any oversight. At first, the most valuable belongings were kept to hand in a bag, later that was forgotten about and at the end of the journey we kept hold of only the most essential items, e.g. I kept with me only my briefcase.

Incidentally I can advise and beg you to put everything you don't actually need on the journey into the baggage. Likewise don't burden Gunars, never mind Dzintra, with any heavy bags. You mustn't worry about them being damaged. When you leave the camp, the baggage you hand over will be safely delivered to the next camp. As for hand luggage labelling, I still haven't got enough examples of what is best, what is least valuable.

For the present, don't throw anything away that might be useful. Even our old iron which I put in the loft, don't throw it away but take it with you. Certain things are expensive: embroidery, dolls, purses and similar things, but bicycles are very cheap. A purse costs 10/- but a second-hand bike, in good condition, you can buy for £2 (just 4 times the cost of a purse). Latvians who work in the camp administration receive £2.10s to £6 per week. On the whole, comparing wages to prices, it seems that here our standard of living will not be worse than in Latvia before the war.

And I want to mention a sad fact that, regarding food rations, we are unhappy. We eat 4 times a day: at lunch we even get 3 courses but the portions are so ridiculously small, at least for us who have been half-starved in Germany for such a long time that hunger tortures me more than before. It doesn't help that the quality is very high and it's also very tasty. Let's hope that, as we get used to things, we will be able to buy some extras, otherwise the future looks bleak. Other than that everything is arranged as comfortably as possible, for example, in the toilet there is special soft paper!

Now a few words about English people. I don't think that, on the whole, they are better or worse than in other countries. But, up to now, we haven't seen examples of the rumoured English standoffishness and coldness towards foreigners. Perhaps to us Displaced Persons, or particularly towards Balts, they have different attitudes. But many examples show civilised English sincerity in really nice actions e.g. when a group of Latvians went to a church service in a Hull church, the Deacon seated them as guests in the front row and, when the vicar was informed, he mentioned them in his sermon, saying that a small group of Latvians had come from their country to the service, that they loved their country no less than the English loved their fatherland but that at the moment they couldn't return home. There followed a prayer for Latvia and the Latvian nation.

After the service many of the parishioners and the vicar wanted to talk to them further. There followed invitations to visit their homes. That's just one episode but there are other examples of interest in Balts. I just stress that often the English are well informed about our nation's circumstances and the role of the Soviet Union and Germany in this.

On average the English person's nature is closer to Latvians than the Germans. The latter is more like the Russians, a person of crowd mentality. The English on the other hand value more individuality, personal liberty and independence, so they don't like their lives and homes to be examined by strangers' eyes, or to attempt to influence them. An often heard saying with the English is "my home is my castle", it seems at all levels. We Latvians are also self-sufficient so we will find fitting in to the English lifestyle will be easier and pleasanter rather than e.g. Russian lifestyle, which after all, even before the Revolution, was that of a crowd person with the raven flock mentality.

What else can I tell you? Just now a Ukrainian has written that in York, where military accommodation was being hurriedly rebuilt for families being brought over to England, a large part is now ready. So I reckon that in June some will be brought over. Overall, here in England, the English themselves see the matter of bringing over the families is an understandable thing that doesn't need discussion. As regards sending parcels to you – I will do it soon, as soon as I acquaint myself with the circumstances and possibilities. They are not as good as I thought earlier, but more about that in the next letter. I wish you all the best, and to yourself lots of kisses. I hope we will see each other soon in the free country of England. Your Valdis.

He writes a letter in the following month in which he refers to the problems and misunderstandings caused by lengthy postal delays.

25th June 1947 Full Sutton, near Stamford Bridge

My dear,
Thank you very much for the newspapers that I got yesterday. From "Greven News", I got to find out how things are your way. Of course, it would be much more pleasant to get this news from yourself but so far I haven't had a single letter from you. I must point out that I wrote to you on the way here and from England a total of 5 letters and this one makes it half a dozen. I imagine you must have written but I haven't received them yet. It's a bit strange, though, that the others in our barrack have received 3 letters, some 2, and I am one of the last ones who is waiting for the first one! Still, I hope to get one soon, then my colleagues won't be able to tease me that my wife has left me and I won't always have to swear that I have the most trustworthy wife in all the Baltic states!

I am still living at Full Sutton and awaiting work. There's not much prospect of getting a Forestry job in the near future, so I applied for agricultural work and, on the 4th of July, I will travel to the agricultural work camp near Sheffield. That is, on the whole, an industrial area but that's not important as sooner or later I will get to work in forestry. In these camps are 50 to 100 people, usually one nationality, and where a large workforce is needed. Pay is 80/- per week from which is deducted 30/- for accommodation and food. This salary is paid by the Ministry of Work, whether or not you work, if no labour is required. It's curious that, in some places, requests for labour are so few that in 3 weeks the men haven't worked for a single day and so a man who came to celebrate midsummer with us was able to buy a gold watch (£9) with the money he had saved. Of course, an absurd situation has developed. Today some of the Latvians from some Polish camp came to work as kitchen staff (!). It seems that they were afraid of the physical work which awaits us in agriculture. I don't remember if I wrote to you that two other Latvians went to another camp as night watchmen (!).

As for our friends, one hasn't got the forestry work they promised him; another is working in a London hospital – "black" work – and writes that he would like to get something more suitable. Another one of our friends and his wife are also left here without work. However, I've started talks with those on the list of the foresters' society to find work for Latvian foresters in England's forestry and have received a favourable reply with some concrete proposals. So I am invited to attend the forestry exhibition in Lincoln next week where the General Secretary of the society promises to put me in touch with the largest private forestry owners in England to get a concrete work offer. I definitely want to make use of this opportunity.

That's enough about work but now something about life in the camp. Food, I think, is the same as I left. We have lost a lot of the appetite we had because of the previous lack of food. We laugh and say we are getting ill *[in Latvian "slims" means "ill"]*. Before, we used to cook an extra pailful of potatoes daily and eat one or two herrings a day; now it's only once every 2 days and then only half a bucket. I personally have recovered enough so that I can make do with the food we are given in the hostel. When we start work, then the food will be increased. Here I want to express how disappointed I am with the communist propaganda[2] which, it seems, has even reached Greven. And, of course, some of the workers who have come to England have written to ask for food parcels to be sent to us in England since we are suffering from famine! My sincere wish is that you and our children could get to this "famine" affected land which I like more every day for the civilised attitude. I don't want to exaggerate but here in a month we feel better than we did in Germany in two years.

In the camp there is a community spirit. I already told you about the 14th November. Immediately after that, our ambassador arrived and gave us a full account of the state of affairs. He is a great optimist regarding the question of if we will be able to return to our own country but only questions how long we will have to stay in exile. That's how strongly he believes in the just nature of our cause. He was particularly pleased with the songs with which his arrival was greeted by the camp or, should I say, the Greven choir.

That was the first time he had heard a Latvian choir in a camp. It has to be said that we of the Greven camp inmates are at the centre. The Anglican service of the 15th June I mentioned was organised by Grevenites including myself. Grevenites organised the choir, the welcome for the ambassador and the address and a Grevenite was chosen for the commission to look into other work possibilities. Grevenites organised the successful outdoor event at midsummer with songs and folk dances to which a large number of English were invited. It was also the Grevenites who composed and sent a memorandum to the Ministry of Labour to grant quicker permits to bring families over to England and other important matters.

There are more Grevenites in Full Sutton than in other camps. Now, with some of us being offered work in other areas, some of the good organisation will fizzle out. In other camps, the Latvian numbers will be too small for proper societies like choirs and drama etc. But when the time comes we will organise social life and Latvian schools.

How are you regarding shoes and other things like clothes? Those things are allowed to be sent to Germany and I want to take advantage of that opportunity as soon as possible. Some goods are forbidden from being sent and many who have done that anyway have had them sent back or were punished by fines or being backlisted.

Until now, I haven't been able to send you anything as I had no spare money from the 5/- a week I got. So I'm fixing radios and building them for the other men and today I got my first payment with which I will be able to buy you a pair of shoes and 4 or 5 pairs of stockings. You will then be able to use them however you want with the knowledge that, when you come to England, you will be able to get as many as you want. Prices for these are low so write to me if you are without shoes, who you gave me sizes for, if the little ones need some (in which case write to me with measurements) and if our friend the Lithuanian woman[3] would like some silk stockings. Then I will try to send you them. As regards the departure of families for England, there is no news other than what I wrote in the last letter. However, we hope to see you over here in August.

Several letters have been received from Latvia in our barrack, one of which was a letter from a mother and some young lady who returned to Latvia from Germany in autumn 1945. The subject of the letter is unarguably – Don't go back on any account. The said young lady, among other things, writes that "a lot of our good people are no longer among us". From the letter, it was revealed that of 5 Legionnaires[4] who, of their free will, returned to Latvia from a prisoner of war camp, only 2 arrived safely but even one of them soon disappeared. There can't be any doubt about what would have happened to us if we had stayed in Latvia.

Well, I will finish now. Next week I travel to a new camp but just write to this address as they will forward our letters. I will await your letter and, for the sake of clarity, I will write an answer to each of your letters, or more correctly, I will write only when I have received a reply from you. If your letter writing is difficult, then ask Dzintra or Gunars to take on your task, or if you haven't got time just write 5 lines! Many kisses to you all! Write soon! Your Valdis. P.S. 11 photos.

[1] Greven was one of 300 Displaced Persons camps for Latvians in West Germany.

[2] The communists disseminated misinformation to persuade refugees who had fled west to return to their homelands now under Soviet Union occupation.

[3] She (like others) provided a valuable service as a black marketeer using goods that were in short supply, like silk stockings, as bartering currency.

[4] Latvians who were forced by the Nazis to serve in the German army.

APPENDIX 5

Valdemars Blankenburgs (V.B.)

This was his Life

1907	Born in Tadaiki, Latvia, then part of the Tsarist Empire.
1914	First World War. Latvia occupied by Germany. V.B. at primary school.
1918	Russian Revolution and Civil War with Communists and German mercenaries in Latvia.
1914-1940	Latvia is independent.
1921	V.B. enrolled in Liepaja Technical College.
1925	V.B. graduates and takes up post as maintenance engineer in Liepaja Coastal Radio Station.
1926	V.B. enrols as student in Latvian State Forestry Academy.
1928	V.B. enrols in the Forestry Faculty, University of Latvia, Riga, and takes up full-time post with the State Electro-technical Factory (VEF) to finance studies.

1929-1944	V.B. takes up post as civil engineer with the Latvian State Forest Department in charge of devising systems of draining forests, wetlands and marshlands within the state forests of Latvia.
1934	Coup d'état. Latvian parliament and political parties suspended.
1934	V.B. marries Elfrida
1939	The Molotov-Ribbentrop Pact. Soviet Union sends fleet and deploys 30,000 troops in Latvia, outnumbering Latvian troops.
1940	100,000 Russian troops occupy Latvia.
1941	Nazis invade and occupy Latvia.
1944	V.B. is Chief Inspector in Latvian Forestry Department.
1944	**November:** V.B. and family flee to Germany as military occupation by Stalinist troops threatens.
1944-1991	**December:** Soviet occupation of Latvia.
1944-1947	150,000 refugees flee from Latvia to Germany and Sweden.
1945	V.B. and his family escape to Germany and become refugees in the British Zone.

1947	**May:** V.B. offered work in the UK under the "European Voluntary Workers" scheme: a 12-month contract involving agricultural work. His family remains in Germany.
1947	**December:** V.B. appointed as Surveyor to Kielder Forest.
1948	**Spring:** The family are reunited at Burnmouth Cottage, Saughtree.
1947-1971	V.B. is Surveyor and later Clerk of works for the Forestry Commission.
1951	**Spring:** V.B. and family move to Kielder.
1968	V.B and his wife move to Bellingham. He founds the Local History Society and serves on the Bellingham Parish Council. He takes thousands of photographs, of which about 10,000 are stored at Woodhorn.
1991	**18th February:** V.B. dies at his home in Bellingham.
1991	**21st August:** Latvia becomes independent after 47 years of Russian occupation.
1992	The ashes of Valdemars Blankenburgs are taken by his wife and son to their final resting place in the new democratic Republic of Latvia.